KEEP FIT EXERCISES FOR KIDS

Carmen Himmerich

KEEP FIT EXERCISES FOR KIDS

ABERDEEN COLLEGE
GORDON LIBRARY

Meyer & Meyer Sport

Original Title
Aschwer/Himmerich: Gymnastik für Kids
© Aachen: Meyer & Meyer, 2002
Translated by Anne Lammert

British Library Cataloguing in Publication Data
A catalogue record for this book is available from the British Library

Carmen Himmerich:
Keep Fit Exercises for Kids
Oxford: Meyer & Meyer Sport (UK) Ltd, 2005
ISBN 1-84126-150-5

© 2005 by Meyer & Meyer Sport (UK) Ltd.
Oxford, Aachen, Olsten (CH), Vienna, Quebec, New York
Adelaide, Auckland, Johannesburg, Budapest
Member of the World
Sports Publishers' Association
Printed and bound: FINIDIR, s. r. o., Český Těšín
E-mail: verlag@m-m-sports.com
www.m-m-sports.com

Contents

Foreword

by Henry Ash, author of the books "Lifelong Success" and "Lifelong Training"

Obesity and posture problems in adults and teenagers have been at the focus of much attention in the past years.

Unfortunately, children younger than 14 years of age are beginning to have similar problems, such as chronic backache and skeletal deformations.

These posture problems and muscular tenseness can have different causes, but one of the main factors is the children's lifestyle.

Lack of physical activity and unbalanced leisure time are the main problems in today's elementary to middle school children.

In these cases, it is essential to educate the public, as well as to provide help to the children and teenagers affected.

Both of these points are being discussed and described with several visual aids in Carmen Himmerich's book. The clear and appealing design of this book, as well as the pictures included, serve the purpose of motivating the children and teenagers to have fun while exercising.

This is just the first step to a successful fight against this underestimated problem.

Coaches, physical education teachers, and you as the parents are responsible for the second step: to help our children to develop a physically healthy body.

This book provides essential information combined with fun to provide your children with the best physical start in life.

I consider myself lucky and proud that my daughter Carmen Himmerich enjoys the satisfaction of being a successful author as much as I do.

Preface

"90% of all children starting school today show signs of postural deficiency, 30% of them already have postural defects". This information hit us on November 28, 2000 from various news channels.

Parent and teacher associations confirm that "sports classes in our schools are being pushed increasingly into the background".

These facts are so alarming that they lead to one single conclusion:

 There must be an urgent improvement in the physical posture of our children and adolescents.

There are three possible paths to follow here:
The first possibility is to look for a sports group which, with the help of a suitable trainer and sports instructor, can counteract the development of such faulty postures.
The second alternative is an appointment with a physiotherapist.
Finally, it is possible within a sports group, this may even be the family, to rectify the oncoming problems oneself through appropriate exercises.

This book aims to offer necessary assistance to all those who are actively involved in combatting postural deficiencies and defects among children and adolescents, whether trainer, sports teacher, sports instructor or helper. This assistance is based on several aspects.

Starting off with a brief theoretical introduction into the relevant basic principles, the positive effects of gymnastic exercises specifically for children and adolescents are then discussed. This is followed by a variety of exercises which, thanks to their brief descriptions and clear illustration, are easy to follow for anyone.

This book will enable children and adolescents to really enjoy movement in the form of gymnastic exercises which are specifically suited to their age groups. At the same time, the exercises are set up in such a way that they are easy for trainers to remember.

Sports and movement are important factors in the developmental process of children and adolescents. As these groups already spend a large part of their day sitting, appropriate compensatory exercises are absolutely essential in order to avoid faulty posture developing in the first place, or at least to effectively counteract these developments in their early stages.

The predominant sitting posture begins at breakfast and continues with the drive to school. The majority of the morning at school is also spent in a sitting position.

Obviously meals are taken sitting down, and they are almost immediately followed by homework activities, which in these modern times of video games and computers are, naturally enough, carried out sitting in front of a computer screen. When this is all over, there must also be enough time left over to watch TV.

A child in the USA watches 25, 000 hours of TV in the first 19 years of his life (Davis/Palladino 1997). This corresponds approximately to a period of three years spent sitting in front of the TV!

The consequences of this unnatural way of life have already brought on a series of problems among children and adolescents, both physical and mental. Included here are incorrrect behavior such as inner and outer restlessness, nervousness and aggression. Postural deficiencies and defects in the locomotor system are further characteristic features of this development. They are already evident among two thirds of all girls and boys although girls are more often affected than boys.

This book shows just exactly how to effectively combat this variety of problems that affects growing girls and boys. The theoretical observations, and in particular, the practical help and advice is aimed at all sports teachers, therapists, trainers and parents who deal with and are responsible for girls and boys between the ages of 6-14 years old.

The contents of this book serve to answer questions and problems, as well as being a reference book for "colorful", interesting training. Athletes and trainers alike can profit from the help offered for identifying inaccuracies when exercises are being carried out for the correction of these errors.

But why keep fit or "gymnastic" exercises? The first chapter concentrates on this central question and explains why gymnastic, keep fit exercises are beneficial even from an early age, and which goals can be achieved through stretching and strengthening exercises. Furthermore, it goes to point out why the frequently neglected stretching exercises are just as important as the strengthening ones.

Functional gymnastics, or, in other words, **anatomically adapted gymnastics**, require **anatomic basic knowledge.** For this reason, some basic anatomic terms are briefly explained, such as skeleton, bones, joints, ligaments, tendons, and muscles. This enables a better understanding of the exercises illustrated later on.

The third chapter looks at the **developmental process from child to adolescent**, not just at individual details, but rather at the child, the adolescent in their entirety.This holistic analysis plays a very important role for a person's growth development in particular.

Children and adolescents are considerably influenced by their family and environment. In their search for their own personal identity and a proper place in society, group sports can exert an extremely positive influence. Motor development and important characteristic patterns of behavior are shaped through group sports.

These facts and explanations should enable the sports instructor to get access to this age group more easily.

Causes of postural deficiencies and defects range from congenital postural defects to lack of exercise and one-sided activities, e.g. playing a musical instrument. It is of utmost importance here to look at the child or adolescent in their entirety. The sports instructor can often get to the bottom of the various causes in a relaxed conversation within the group or with the individual child.

Good timing and layout of a gymnastics lesson specifically for children and adolescents should enable an easier sequence of events in the lesson. A 'circuit' is of advantage for taking account of all aspects and factors within a gymnastics session.

Before moving on to practical exercises, the next chapter offers **tips and sample exercises for warming up**. Preparing the body serves as a basis of any sports activity in order to prevent any injuries occurring, and secondly to encourage the children to have fun moving about. General warming up possibilities are shown here, as well as some sample "breaking the ice" games.

The warm up is followed by **functional gymnastics**, starting off with the foot and calf muscles, and moving on to all important muscle groups in the body up as far as whole body gymnastics.

The individual, partner, and group exercises shown here illustrate both the strengthening and corresponding stretching required by all major muscle groups.

Practical help is also offered for identifying possible errors or compensatory movements.

Being able to identify **disturbances in balance, coordination and perception** is very important for training instructors working with children and adolescents, as participants missing out on these basic motor experiences require a lot at patience and empathy.

These problems are becoming more and more common due to children's and adolescents' leisure activities being frequently too monotonous these days. For this reason, this book provides you with exercises for balance training, coordination training, as well as for physical and spatial perception.

Good, well-developed coordinative skills are needed for balancing or riding a bike. The correct perception of such terms as "above", "below", "right" and "left" is being trained of the same time.

The exercise section is then followed up by a selection of **exercise programs for each specific age group**.

Games with that extra something are presented in the next chapter. These are divided up into community, team and chasing activities. They can be used with various age groups, and involve a lot of fun and variety.

The book finishes off with some **advice on sports injuries,** explaining the necessary first aid measures in each case. This chapter also looks at preventative measures, and the most frequent damage caused by overstrain.

A healthy diet during the years of development is very important. All athletes should possess basic knowledge of this.

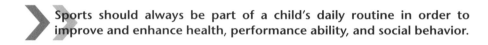 **Sports should always be part of a child's daily routine in order to improve and enhance health, performance ability, and social behavior.**

1 WHY GYMNASTIC EXERCISES FOR YOUNG CHILDREN AND ADOLESCENTS?

We differentiate between three target groups from now on. To keep things simple, they will be referred to as follows:

- **Kids:** for children aged 6-8 years
- **Big kids:** for children aged 9-11 years
- **Teens:** for adolescents aged 12-14 years.

The problems facing children and adolescents have already been pointed out in the foreword and preface. Counteractive measures from an early stage are thus imperative here in order to combat the common postural deficiencies and threatening postural defects. This can be achieved in the five following ways:

Maintaining flexibility	(Chapter 1.1)
Strengthening the support apparatus	(Chapter 1.2)
Improving balance	(Chapter 11)
Optimizing coordination	(Chapter 12)
Perception training	(Chapter 13)

When all aspects are accounted for in a gymnastics lesson, this does not merely lead to an improvement in these five skills but also encourages the fun aspect of moving about. The deciding factors, however, are a maintenance of flexibility and strengthening of the support apparatus, i.e. **functional gymnastic exercises**.

Functional gymnastics thus combines both strengthening and stretching exercises. Such exercises are anatomically adapted to the extent that those muscles prone to shortening are stretched, and those muscles prone to weakening are strengthened. Today's typical problems, such as lack of movement and incorrect sitting behavior, are also accounted for in the exercises selected. In order to have a simple structure in the lesson, it is a good idea to begin with strengthening exercises, and finish off with stretching exercises, so as to bring the activated muscles back to their original length. In certain forms of sports, such as artistic gymnastics, ballet or jazz dance, it is necessary to both start off and finish up with stretching exercises. Stretching at the beginning is extremely important to be able to carry out specific exercises which require a large degree of flexibility. In functional gymnastics, however, stretching exercises after the strengthening section are enough.

Keeping in line with the holistic treatment of children and adolescents, it is important to take account of the frequently neglected inner balance, i.e. mental factors. Just as flexing and stretching muscles work together when running, in the same way, a complete person is made up of physical and mental components.

1.1 Maintaining Flexibility

What is meant by **flexibility** or **movability?**
    Flexibility refers to the degree of movement between the working partners of a joint (e.g. elbow joint) or of several joints (spinal column). The scope of these movements depends on the stretchability of the elastic structures i.e. of the muscles, ligaments, tendons, form of joint and muscle strength.

Even in the **Kids** and **Big Kids** age group, muscular dysbalances are diagnosed more and more often these days, and can be attributed to many factors. On the one hand, it is the result of a striking lack of movement among children and adolescents; on the other hand, it is the one-sided leisure activities. For this reason it is important to strengthen the weakened muscles, and to return the shortened muscles to their original length with stretching exercises, so as not to hinder mobility.

Every muscle has an individual basic level of tautness from which it can be actively shortened or stretched. Strong muscles, such as the knee-bending muscles on the rear thigh, have a high basic level of tautness, and for this reason are more prone to "shrinkage".

A well-stretched muscle is also a source of protection in the case of sudden high loads, e.g. jumps or quick changes of direction. Suspension is better,and this in turn, prevents any difficulties occurring in muscles and tendons.

Stretching in **the Teen age group** is of great importance because of the increased pace of growth throughout puberty. This growing phase and the continuous changes in the body's constitution lead to unfavourable force and lever relationships.

Due to the change in body height and body mass, frequently accompanied by lack of movement, one-sided activities, and in some cases initial weight problems, the muscles of the posture and locomotor apparatus tend to shorten.

For this reason strengthening exercises should always be followed up by suitable stretching exercises, so as to stimulate both qualities of the muscle (strength and extent of movement).

Every person with a good understanding of his body knows that unpleasant feeling in the rear thigh and calf muscles after a long car drive. It's often the case that one unconsciously starts stretching these muscles during a break. It's exactly the same for children and adolescents.

Having sat monotously for hours, the origin and insertion of certain muscles are permanently so near to each other that this leads to a number of unpleasant side effects.

Muscle shortening occurs in:

- **the calf muscles**
- **the rear thigh muscles**
- **the hip muscles**
- **the pectoral muscles, and sometimes**
- **the abdominal muscles and**
- **the neck muscles.**

In the gymnastic section of this book, stretching exercises for all the areas mentioned above are explained and illustrated. Most of these exercises can be carried out easily and in a playful way while still achieving the goal of maintaining or improving the ever-important muscle flexibility.

A few general points about stretching beforehand:

Why stretching is so important even for children and adolescents:

- It prevents muscles from losing their flexibility.

- It compensates for lack of movement and for one-sided activities.

- It prevents muscular dysbalance during the growing phase of puberty.

- It compensates for the basic tautness of various muscles.

- Sudden peaks in load have a better suspension.

Aims of adapted stretching are:

- To avoid muscular dysbalance.

- To maintain and bring back normal muscle length.

- To improve muscle blood flow and muscle metabolism.

- To convey a better body awareness.

- Better regeneration after intensive muscular strengthening.

- Mental relaxation.

1.2 Strengthening the Support Apparatus

The idea behind strengthening exercises is to improve strength endurance, i.e. the body's ability to fight against fatigue after a long strength performance.

Regular strengthening exercises enable our body to build up a protective muscle "corset". Two to three times a week can be recommended here; however, improvements can be achieved even through intensive training once a week.These exercises, when correctly carried out, stabilize the bones, joints and ligaments, and make everybody (not just children and adolescents) more resistant to mechanical strain (e.g in the case of a fall).

With **kids, big kids and teens**, trunk strengthening exercises should never become a "training dictation", but rather always take particular consideration of their movement urge and play instinct. The trainer must take account of their desire to move and play if he wants to give a lesson that is attractive and rich in variety. You cannot compare a group of children and adolescents with a group of calm, interested and disciplined adults. This specific aspect is therefore repeatedly taken into consideration throughout this book.

Between the age of 11 and 14, a child moves from being a child to an adolescent; for this reason the exercises should be more frequently carried out with a partner and in a playful form. One should also try to incorporate certain adult functional gymnastic exercises into the **teen** program.

Why is sitting so bad for **kids, big kids, and teens** in particular?
    The reason for these problems is that **active** sitting is neglected or only kept up for a short time. When sitting actively, the feet are on the floor wider apart from each other than the hips; at the same time, the pelvis is tilted forward, and the chin and shoulders are moved back slightly. This sitting position involves less strain on the spinal column, muscles and ligaments, but the appropriate trunk muscles are necessary for this. Those persons who are not accustomed to sitting like this will soon "feel" this active sitting position after a few minutes.

For this reason, they move out of the strenous position, give up tensing the stomach and back muscles, and so muscular security disappears. They end up in a **passive** sitting position which is more of a hanging of the ligaments.

Active sitting　　　　　　　　　　　*Passive sitting*

Children and adolescents sit around passively for hours, and this not only leads to a shortening of the pectoral and abdominal muscles, but also to a weakness in the abdominal and back muscles. If this posture is kept up for years without any counteractive gymnastic measures, it may not only lead to postural anomaly, but also to intervertebral disk lesions, disorders of the digestive tract and restrictions in breathing, so it's worth remembering to keep up good posture when sitting.

Prone position is also beneficial when reading or learning as the abdominal muscles are stretched in this position, and the spinal column is also in an outstretched position. In order to avoid overstretching of the lumbar spine, it is a good idea to push a cushion under one's stomach.

For the long term, however, it is only possible to achieve relief in the passive locomotor system through appropriate strengthening exercises and corresponding stretching exercises.

Extreme postural defects among 6-14 year-olds, such as scoliosis (sideward warping of the spine), can no longer be rectified with good gymnastic exercises in a group. A visit to an orthopedic doctor is to be recommended here followed by numerous sittings with a physiotherapist.

A special exercise program is set up here, based on the weaknesses prevailing, and this is to be supplemented with a home exercise program.

Regular strengthening of the supporting apparatus prevents the occurrence of all the above-mentioned problems, thus saving the person concerned a great deal of time and money for necessary therapy treatment later on.

A popular alternative to carrying out the exercise programs alone, as illustrated in the second part of this book, is taking part in regular group lessons. These are offered by clubs, schools, or other organizations, and are run by experienced sports instructors. Exercising in a group is, on the one hand, certainly more motivating and definitely much more fun; on the other hand, one is bound to the times given for these sessions.

Why strengthening is so important even for children and adolescents.

- For the build-up of a protective muscle corset.

- For a higher resistance ability to mechanical strains.

- To prevent muscular dysbalance during the growing phase in puberty.

- To relieve the passive locomotor system.

- To improve body posture and sitting behavior.

Aims of strengthening are:

▢ To avoid muscular dysbalance.

▢ To optimize body posture.

▢ To stabilize the passive locomotor system.

▢ To enhance muscle blood flow and muscle metabolism.

▢ To improve strength endurance.

2 THE COMPLEX LOCOMOTOR SYSTEM

The human locomotor system is built up out of a **passive** and **active** apparatus, and these combine to form a functional unit.

The **passive** apparatus of locomotion is the human skeleton; the **active** apparatus of locomotion refers to our muscular system.

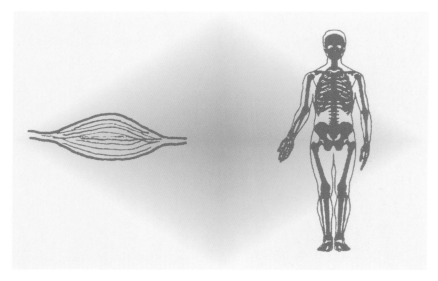

Active apparatus of locomotion
(muscle)

Passive apparatus of locomotion
(skeleton)

It is of elementary importance for a person's health to stabilize the passive apparatus of locomotion (skeleton) with the help of the active apparatus (muscles), thus protecting it from faulty developments.

If one part is defective or out of order, e.g. a bone fracture, this immediately has a negative influence on the other part. In this case, it is mainly a shortening and weakening of the surrounding muscles with corresponding negative effects in the form of limitation in mobility.

2.1 What Belongs to the Passive Apparatus of Locomotion?

The **passive** apparatus of locomotion refers to the **human skeleton**, the **framework**, and is made up of the following components:

- **Bones:** Bones make up the body's framework to withstand a muscle's entire pulling force, enabling us to stand up erect. The firmness of these bones depends mainly on daily loads, nutrition, however, plays an equally important role.

- **Joints:** Joints are connections between two or more bones. They are covered with cartilage, and thus, represent the mobile parts of the skeleton.

- **Cartilage:** Cartilage forms a protective layer over the joints, so that the joint "partners" are able to move almost free of friction. Regular movement of the joints is, therefore, imperative as there is no blood flow to cartilage; it is passively looked after through diffusion instead. Cartilage can also be found in the embryonic skeleton, as well as in the spine and miniscus.

- **Ligaments:** Ligaments serve to hold together those parts of the skeleton which move together e.g. the cruciate ligamants of the knee.

- **Tendons:** Tendons are the combining pieces between muscles and bones which have to withstand up to a muscle's entire pulling force.

The skeleton is also there to protect the brain, spinal marrow and inner organs. The bones carry our body's weight, and are thus, an anchor to the skeleton muscles attached in each case.

The osseous (bone) structure of a child is subject to permanent changes in length, width and general composition. Due to pulling and pushing impulses on the skeleton, cartilage is converted into bone, so that the body can adapt to increases in weight and strain.

Body structure changes several times at a child's age; it starts off with the normal or physiological baby's round back, which later, due to standing and walking, soon changes to a curved spinal column.

The curves of the spine are known as **kyphosis** and **lordosis**. While kyphosis refers to the normal backward curving of the spine in the area of the dorsal spine, lordosis illustrates the forward curving in the cervical and lumbar spine areas.

The leg axis continues to change, away from the toddler's bandy legs to knocked knees at kindergarten age, which appears as a result of the increased amount of pressure on the inside of the knees. However, this axis returns to normal again by the age of 6 or 7.

Up to schoolgoing age, the initial flat feet develop into plantar arches, and these play a vital role as a shock absorber for the knees, hips, and spine.

Particularly in this phase when many changes are taking place within the body, it is advisable to motivate children to take part in sports, as regular activities improve bone growth, bone structure, and mineral content, all of which in turn lead to better stability of the passive apparatus of locomotion.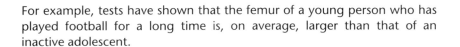

For example, tests have shown that the femur of a young person who has played football for a long time is, on average, larger than that of an inactive adolescent.

2.2 What Belongs to the Active Apparatus of Locomotion?

With the **active** apparatus of locomotion, we mean the the **skeletal muscles** connected to the bones of the passive apparatus by **tendons**.

The muscles are under the control of the brain, and they react to nerve impulses with a contraction. The bone experiences a shift in emphasis via the tendons, and this results in a movement.

A muscle is able to adapt to outer conditions relatively well. The thickness of the muscle fibers can be increased through regular training, which in turn causes an increase in muscular strength. Regular, well held stretching intervals can similarly lengthen a muscle, and this in turn can cause a rise in the muscle's scope of movement.

However, muscles are not only there for the sake of movement, but also for stability and posture, as mentioned in Chapter 1.

The building component of a skeletal muscle is the crossways striped muscle fiber. This is a giant frame, with a length of up to 15-30cm, and a diameter of approx. 0.1mm. One differentiates between two types of muscle fiber: white fibers which tire quickly, and the endurant red fibers.

Phasial muscles are composed of white fibers, and are there for speed, strength, and mobility; they are prone to weakness. Included here are posterior muscles, foot-lifting muscles, and those muscles between the shoulderblades.

Tonic muscles are made up from the red fibers, and are slow to fatigue, but are prone to shortening. Muscles in this category would be the pectoral, hip-flexing, knee-bending and calf muscles.

In order to activate both types of muscle fiber, every session of gymnastic exercises should contain strengthening and stretching elements.

3 DEVELOPMENT – FROM A CHILD TO AN ADOLESCENT

What is development?

A growing child does not only get heavier, bigger and older, but also cleverer, more dextrous and more confident. He captures his environment; he becomes independent and adapts himself more and more to his surroundings. In order to complete this process of adaptation, he needs to practice using his muscles and nerves from early on.

In the same way, a newborn child learns to taste, smell, see, hear and feel what is going on around him. These impressions of the senses are stored in the brain, so that they can be recognized and identified again later. Taking in and dealing with impressions from our environment is only one side of the learning experience, we must also learn to analyze this environment through active behavior.

With the help of movement organs, a child can extend what he vaguely took in with his senses, through learning and experimenting, which is basically the opinion of E. J. Kiphard (1996).

Every child is born with genetic features such as size, weight and constitution. Environmental factors such as healthy nutrition, proneness to illnesses, and general parental care, all have a considerable influence on a child's growth and development.

Appropriate continuous movement during the growing phase is what's required for bones, tendons and muscle tissue to develop as they should. Regular movement does not only improve bone density, but also the bone's mineral content. Lack of movement and exercise can limit the potential growth of the body and its organs.

Children who are shown to possess an optimal level of physical fitness normally attain the maximal level of development and growth. They are less prone to emotional disturbances, are normally better able to adapt, and are in general very open-minded.

The following factors have a considerable influence on this development:
- **The active family:** This always has a positive influence on the child or adolescent.
- **The circle of friends:** Sports activities are frequently carried out together during child and adolescent age.
- **The living area:** In rural regions, in some cases, very few suitable sports associations are available; in the cities, however, there are many more sports associations.
- **Age:** At a young age, sport, i.e. active movement, is frequently replaced with passive activities and an excessive interest in media.

3.1 Motor Development

Motor development already begins at newborn and infant age. Each child is an individual, developing according to his own personal pattern, and this is influenced by his background and surroundings. The fact that many children completely skip the crawling stage, for example, shows that this development does not always take the same course of events.

According to Frankenberg in Davis/Palladino (1997), motor development among children in the USA is as follows:

Skill:	Age :
Rolling or turning	5.5 months
Sitting without support	7 months
Standing with support	8.5 months
Grasping with finger and thumb	10.5 months
Free standing	14 months
Walking without assistance	15 months
Climbing stairs	22 months
Kicking a ball	23.5 months

From the ages of two to six years, children learn basic movements such as running, jumping, hopping, climbing, rolling, swinging, pushing, pulling, throwing, and catching.

At this age, it is important to remember not to set the performance demands up too high. Sports and games must always be adapted according to the child's age if they are to be successful.

A short example here:

A well meaning father, bought his 5 year-old daughter stilts. He is not aware that his daughter at this age does not possess the necessary balance and body control. The attempts to walk with these large stilts are a failure; the father gets impatient as his daughter simply can't manage it. It ends up in tears! If, however, the child had been provided with the mini-stilts suitable for her age (tins with strings), both father and child would certainly have had a lot of fun.

Kids of 6-9 years continue improving the skills they have already learned; height is an advantage for neither boys nor girls, according to Hall/Lee in Kirchner (1981).

At this age children are able to combine movements, such as running and jumping, catching and throwing.

Generally, **kids** are

- very creative.
- fascinated by rhythm and music.
- interested in improvements and repetition.
- enthusiastic about organized and challenging competitive and team games.
- adventurous, are not afraid.
- willing to take part in cooperative activities and partner exercises.

From the age of nine years onwards, big kids and teens are able to carry out advanced activites which require a certain degree of skilfulness. They are particularly ambitious when working on improvements in their sporting activities.

The most popular sports activities for **big kids and teens** are as follows:

- Various forms of dance such as ballet, jazz dance, hip-hop.
- Specific gymnastic exercises such as handstand, flip-flop.
- Ball games e.g. soccer, basketball, volleyball.
- Combat sports such as judo and karate.
- Athletics.
- Swimming.

Up to puberty, a continuous climb in strength abilities among boys and girls (teens) can be noticed. However, due to the male hormone testosterone, boys experience a considerably stronger increase in strength than girls.

This hormonal influence enhances muscle growth, muscles generally grow in size, and this leads to a further rise in strength. The girls make no progress in this area during this time period, or sometimes even deteriorate in performance.

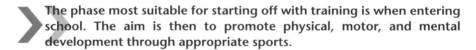 **The phase most suitable for starting off with training is when entering school. The aim is then to promote physical, motor, and mental development through appropriate sports.**

3.2 Characteristic Forms of Behavior

It is important for anyone wishing to work successfully with children and adolescents to know what particular forms of behavior are to be expected in this sports group. When he knows this, only then is it possible for a sports instructor to take adequate account of these factors, and thus, set the basis for potentially successful work together.

For simplicity's sake, the numerous amounts of these various patterns of behavior are listed below.

One must take adequate account of the following demands and forms of behavior that are typical for kids, big kids and teens:

Six years of age

Characteristic forms of behavior:
- Restless, ambitious, overactive, easily tired.
- Self-presumptuous, aggressive, always want to be first.
- Less cooperative than at the age of five, boasting.
- Learn best through active participation.
- Brief periods of interest only.
- Have difficulties making decisions.
- Group activities are popular, however interests between boys and girls begin to drift apart.
- Frequent overexaggeration of things.

Particular needs:
- Support, praise, warmth, and a lot of patience from adults.
- Opportunities for many activities and sports.
- Time with friends.
- Responsibility, but without pressure or complicated decisions.
- Assistance when learning acceptable manners and habits.

Seven years of age

Characteristic forms of behavior:
- Sensitive regarding other children's and adults' attitudes and feelings.
- Boys' and girls' interests develop diametrically.
- Energetic, but quickly fatigued, restless and fidgety.
- Often dreamy and absent.
- Scattered thinking, best learning success with activities.
- Careful and self-critical.
- Talkative, tend to overexaggerate, fight verbally instead of physically.
- Enjoy music, nature stories, comics, TV, cinema.
- Are able to take on a little responsibility.
- Are concerned about right and wrong standpoints.
- Elementary understanding of time and money.

Particular needs:
- To assume the right combination of responsibility and maintain support.
- Wild games and jumping around in a playground with adults.
- A peaceful relationship with adults.
- Yearning for warmth and personal support.

Eight years of age

Characteristic forms of behavior:
- "Don't care" attitude, being loud, enjoy arguing.
- Alert, friendly and interested in other people.
- Very sensitive to criticism.
- Ambitious, cocky rather than careful, high rate of accidents.
- Group formation, best friends are of the same sex.
- During conflicts, trust in peers rather than adults.
- Understanding of time and value of money.
- Interested in group activities among children, but also in joint activities with adult supervision.

Particular needs:
- Praise and encouragement from adults.
- Reminders about responsibility.
- Guidance and promotion of interests.
- A best friend.
- Experiences and identification with a group of peers.
- Leisure group activities, sports in particular.

Nine and ten years of age

Characteristic forms of behavior:
- Responsible, sensible, reliable, accurate recognition of right and wrong.
- Strong group identity.

- Perfectionist attitude, want to do everything properly, lose interest however through adult pressure.
- Spend a lot of time in conversation and discussion.
- Enjoy criticising adults.
- Argue about justice in sport and games.

Particular needs:
- Active, wild games.
- Friends, group membership.
- Dexterity exercises but without pressure.
- Books, depending on interests.
- Responsibility.

Eleven to thirteen years of age (phase before puberty)

Characteristic forms of behavior:
- The girls are generally taller and heavier than boys of the same age as they enter puberty two years earlier than boys on average.
- Boys experience rapid muscle growth and in some cases an enormous but changeable appetite.
- Big differences in the maturing process of 11-13 year-olds.
- Group membership is still important.
- Interest in team games, house pets, TV, comics, films.
- Annoying and teasing between boys and girls.
- Clumsiness, lethargy, often a result of quick or uneven growth.
- Opinion of peers is more valuable than adults' opinions.
- Frequent exaggerated criticism, rebellious and uncooperative behavior.
- Strong interest in money.

Particular needs:
- Understanding of physical and emotional changes.
- Opportunities of more responsibility and independence.
- Affection from others.
- Adult humor.
- Non-critical adults.

Fourteen to eighteen years of age (puberty, adolescence) ────────────

Characteristic forms of behavior:
- A difficult age for both the young adults and sports instructors; further weight gains, enormous appetite, completion of bone growth.
- Emotional instability in combination with "going for the extreme".
- " I know everything" attitude.
- Return to nailbiting, daydreaming.
- Yearning for idols.
- Fear of "not being popular".
- Oversensitiveness and self-pity.
- Strong identification with the idolized adult.
- Groups become cliques.
- Outer appearance becomes very important.

Particular needs:
- Acceptance among peers.
- Understanding of friendships with and attitudes towards the opposite sex.
- A feeling of security, as adolescents are looking for dependence and indepence at the same time.
- Opportunities to make their own decisions.
- Earning and saving money.

When the various above-mentioned needs of the children and adolescents are taken into account in gymnastic exercises, one can expect to have an improved level of motivation, and better prospects of success with the participants.

For example, topics dealing with nature and animals are interesting for a **kids** group, whereas the **big kids** group enjoys doing dexterity exercises; **teens,** on the other hand, are interested in the latest music, and this can be successfully incorporated into the warm-up phase.

3.3 The Holistic Method of Observation

When doing gymnastics work with children and adolescents, one must make sure to take into account both motor development and characteristic forms of behavior. Only those trainers who try to address the participants in their individual entirety in these decisive years of development will be able to gain more influence, and work successfully within his exercise and training groups.

Thus, for this section of the population, it is not enough to merely look at functional gymnastics or at the social components only; the individual in his entirety should be the central focus of the instructor's attention.

The human body in its social dimension serves not only as an instrument of expression, but also offers eye and skin contact. Satisfaction and being at one with one's own body is a basic requirement for a person's self-confidence and self-esteem.

The feeling of one's own value, also known as a positive self-image, develops from an early age.

The more recognition a child receives due to his posture, overall physical appearance, and motor activity, the more balanced his emotional wellbeing will be, and the more harmonious he will be with himself, and the world.

For this reason, it is clear that those children who do not feel acknowledged and accepted in their physicality are particularly prone to having self-doubts and minority complexes. This is especially true for children and adolescents with weight problems (over-, underweight), and other physical deficiencies or disturbances as these problems are clearly evident in normal day-to-day life, and during sports activities in particular.

Therefore, when working with children and adolescents who have problems with their self-esteem, it is extremely important to convey a sense of achievement in regards to their progress in physical fitness and performance ability.

4 CAUSES OF POSTURAL DEFECTS AND DEFICIENCIES

The term **postural deficiency** refers to a muscular weakness of the support apparatus. Without gymnastic countermeasures this weakness can, after a while, lead to **postural decline** or a **postural defect**. Painful muscular tension, which in some cases already requires medical treatment, frequently accompanies postural deficiencies, and indicates the real problem when it's too late.

There are many different reasons for bad posture: from genetic deformities to bone illnesses and incorrect foot positions. The latter are very common among children, and have a negative effect on the knees, hips and spine.

The principal causes of postural defects and deficiencies today, however, are due to:

- lack of movement
- bad sitting behavior
- one-sided leisure behavior of children and adolescents

That the frightening lack of exercise and bad sitting habits over a long period of time can result in postural deficiencies and defects does not need to be explained any more at this stage. But, the fact that one-sided leisure activities can also be a cause can be seen in the following true example:

A ten year-old boy enters a physiotherapy practice in order to receive individual therapy for his postural weakness. During the first session, it comes out by coincidence in the middle of a relaxed conversation, that his whole family is very musical, and that he, too, is an enthusiastic cellist. At my request, this very diligent cellist showed me his typical sitting position. The cause of his problems soon became clear to me. His daily practicing of about 2-3 hours in a position which is quite unfriendly to the spine, and this over a time span of approx. three years, has led to his rounded back and a sideward warping of his spinal column. After intensive daily gymnastic exercises, and a correction of his sitting position while playing cello, his posture was returned to normal after six months.

However, regular compensatory exercises are still necessary to prevent the defect from coming back.

So, it is clear that individual talks with children and adolescents, even during a group exercise, enable important causal research. This can, for example, occur in the stretching phase. With this simple procedure, it is often possible to identify existing or looming postural defects in good time. At the same time, one can give individual tips and advice in a very personal way.

A long-term postural weakness results in the skeleton being ossified in its incorrect position, thus causing false postures such as a rounded back, hollow back, or a flat back. These are illustrated below; the normal back in comparison:

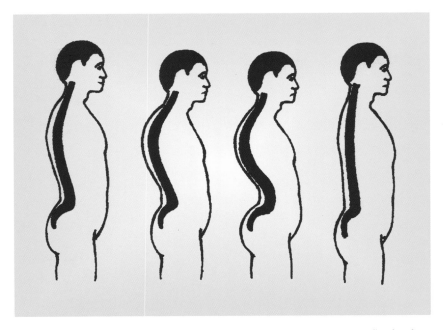

Normal back   *rounded back*   *hollow back*   *flat back*

A rounded back position causes the thorax and shoulders to droop towards the front. This frequently happens when sitting down, as in the passive sitting position described in Chapter 1.2. Muscle shortening occurs here in the chest and stomach muscles, whereas the back muscles are overstretched and weakened. A correction of posture is achieved by stretching the shortened muscles and strengthening the back muscles.

A participant with a **hollow rounded back** also tries to compensate for his rounded back by tilting the pelvis to the front, i.e. strong lordosis. The muscular situation is very similar to above; however, in this case, his abdominal and posterior muscles have to be strengthened as well, so as to compensate for the exaggerated lordosis (hollow position) in his spinal column.

A child with a flat back has reduced oscillation in his spinal column, i.e. reduced kyphosis in the area of the thoracic spine (chest), as well as diminished lordosis in the cervical and lumbar spinal area. Stretching of the abdominal, hip-stretching and rear thigh muscles is what is needed here, as these muscles counteract the physiological lumbar lordosis. A strengthening program for the back muscles complements the gymnastic exercises; see the exercises in Chapter 8.

5 TIMING AND CONTENT OF A GYMNASTIC LESSON SPECIFICALLY FOR CHILDREN AND ADOLESCENTS

An interesting and successful gymnastics lesson with children and adolescents must fulfill the following three different tasks:

1. Prevention of false postures.
2. Eradication of postural deficiencies and postural defects.
3. Fun and pleasure doing the necessary exercises, and taking part in sports.

These tasks can be fulfilled when we take into account the following eight points:

1. **Requirements:**
   ■ Clothing suitable for sports: comfortable sports pants and top, non-slip socks.
   Sports shoes are not obligatory for functional gymnastics.
   Foot gymnastics should always be done barefoot, so as to further encourage the plantar arch.
   ■ Optimization of route conditions, perhaps through car sharing.

2. **Greeting:**
   ■ With a new group, it is always a good idea to promote personal contact through "getting to know games".
   ■ Introduce starting rituals when suitable, e.g. for young children, forming a circle holding hands and saying "Hi, hello, how are you?" together.

3. **Warm-up:**
   ■ The aim of the warm-up is to motivate the children, and satisfy their natural movement urge.
   ■ Warm-up exercises should be varied and creative in form.
   Sample exercises for greeting and warming up can be found in Chapter 6.

4. Main section:
- This section should consist of functional stretching and strengthening exercises in the form of playful individual, partner and group exercises. See Chapters 7, 8, 9 and 10.

5. End section
- Various game forms are possible. One should comply with the participants' suggestions and wishes in the process here as much as possible. Exercises for this section are in Chapter 11,12 and 15.

6. Relaxation phase
- Before the children and adolescents leave the room, it's a good idea to include a brief relaxation phase. In contrast to the liveliness up to now, this relaxation phase can be used perfectly for perception games and exercises for perception. (Chapter 13).

7. Finish
- Equipment is tidied up as a group together.
- A short feedback from the group is important for finding out what the group really enjoyed, and what was not so popular.
- When another five minutes are left, it is a good opportunity to have a little discussion about some practical elements like nutrition. (Examples of this in Chapter 17.)

8. Saying goodbye
- The session ends with a nice goodbye, and perhaps some exciting details about the next gymnastics session.

The exact time allocation of a gymnastics session obviously depends on the time allowed in the first place. If one has 60 minutes for a lesson, one could then recommend the following cycle:

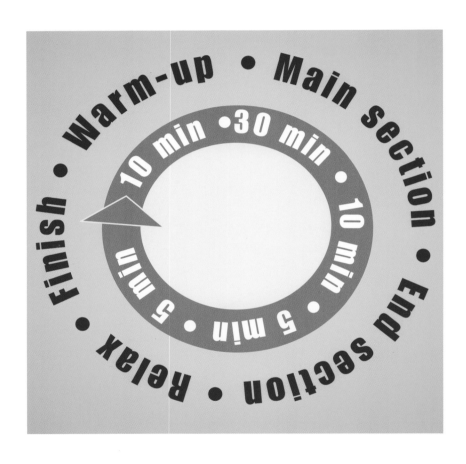

6 TIPS AND SAMPLE EXERCISES FOR WARMING UP

Imagination and inventiveness are eminently important, particularly in a group with children and adolescents, as otherwise boredom or lack of interest may develop.

In the greeting phase, getting-to-know-games have proven to be particularly successful, as they allow scope for fun and creativity.

6.1 Greeting or Getting-to-know Games

Shaking hands
The group wanders through the room, shaking hands with every participant who comes towards them, and introducing themselves by their first name. After this round, the activity is carried out again the other way round, so that each participant has to say the other person's name.

Numerous variations are possible here, such as:
- High five
- Curtsey
- Nod of the head
- Hint of a hand kiss
- Pretend to raise one's hat etc.

Children often have their own interesting ideas, and the instructor should always have an open ear for them.

Remembering names
The group stands in a circle. The instructor throws a gymnastic ball to a child or adolescent, and says his first name. This introduction process with the ball is continued until every participant has said his name once. Then, the ball should be thrown again in the same order as before but this time the person throwing the ball must try to say the first name of the person catching it.

An easier variation of this e.g. for 6-year-old children, is as follows:
    After everyone has said his first name as in the exercise above, the ball can then be thrown to anyone in the circle whose name one has managed to remember.

Introducing partners
The children or adolescents form pairs, and introduce each other to the rest of the group. As well as the name, one can mention hobbies, favorite color, movie, animal etc. etc.

Star and journalist
"Star and journalist" is also an exercise for pairs. The couple practice their interview first, before presenting it to the group. One child is a journalist, the other a star. The sports instructor should limit the amount of questions to be asked in the interview.

6.2 Warm-up Phase

Warming up is essential as the muscles have to get accustomed to the oncoming work involved in strengthening and stretching exercises. The aim of a warm-up phase is to improve the blood flow and metabolism of the muscles, at the same time the circulation is activated and the body temperature rises. The group has to gradually get used to each other, and creativity and liveliness ought to be allowed.

Walking and running variations are suitable for the beginning; it is often a lot of fun when each participant demonstrates a particular exercise.
Below is a list of the many possible variations:

Go around the room and
- consciously roll the foot from the heel to the big toe.
- walk like a stork.
- walk only on the balls of the feet.
- walk only on the heels.
- walk backwards.
- walk sideways using the cross step.

■ pluck apples. All participants stretch up high, and then crouch down low to place the apples into a basket, and then go on to the next tree.

Run/jog through the room and
■ do whatever arm movements one feels like, such as circling etc.
■ clap to indicate a change in direction.
■ clap to freeze all other participants to stone.
■ touch the bottom with the heels.
■ hop or skip along.
■ carry out a sideward gallop.
■ do the cross step.

When working with these age groups, it is also possible to use simple aids, e.g. newspapers, scarves, which the participants can bring to the lesson themselves.

Scarves can be included in the warm-up phase for carrying out arm movements (swing, circles or figure eights) during the walking or running exercises. They are also good for exercises set to music. It's particularly fascinating to see all the colors in motion within the group.

Newspapers are a welcome change to the normal materials used in gymnastics. The following variations are suitable for the warm-up phase:
■ Walking/running through the rain with the newspaper spread out over one's head.
■ While walking, pretend to be reading the newspaper.
■ Folding up the newspaper, and balancing it on one's head.
■ Tucking the newspaper under one's arm, and then skipping and hopping.
■ Each participant should try and see if the newspaper stays stuck to his stomach when he quickly runs around the room .
■ At the end, everyone rolls his newspaper into a ball, and tries to transport this into the waste paper basket without using his hands.

The oncoming Chapters 7-13 look at the main section of a gymnastics session.

7 EXERCISES FOR STRENGTHENING AND STRETCHING THE LOWER EXTREMITIES

Chapters 1.1 and 1.2 already dealt with the importance of stretching and strengthening. When carrying out exercises, one should generally pay attention to the following points.

Important aspects of stretching exercises:

- Only do stretching when already warmed up.
- A pulling sensation in the muscles is allowed, however, pain is to be avoided.
- Breathing should be kept steady.
- Stretching duration should be between 15 and 30 seconds in each case.
- 2-4 repetitions.
- No springing or bouncing allowed (this automatically causes muscle contraction).

Important aspects of strengthening exercises:

- Isometric strengthening exercises should be kept up for 6-10 seconds.
- One should continue to breathe calmly during isometric exercises.
- At least five repetitions of all strengthening exercises.
- When using one's own body weight for strengthening exercises, one should breathe out when the strain is at its strongest.

General rules:

For pair exercises, it is a good idea to put children of about the same size together.

When carrying out certain exercises, it is advisable to use gymnastic mats to lie on, as this is both kinder to the joints, and reduces the risk of accidents, for example when using dynaboards or beams.

7.1 Strengthening and Stretching Foot and Calf Muscles

STRENGTHENING EXERCISES

Exercise 1: **Toe Figures**

- **Aim:** To strengthen toe lifting muscles, and muscles in the soles of the feet
- **Type:** 1a: exercise by oneself, 1b: group exercise
- **Equipment:** Ropes (1 rope per participant)

1a: Starting position:
While standing around in a circle, every participant has a rope lying in front of him.

Procedure:
Only the feet are allowed to be used. Depending on the age group, the participants are to make figures with the rope by grasping it with their toes "clawed". Snails, squares, letters, numbers or figures such as houses or trees can be given as tasks.

1b:
After these individual exercises, it is a good idea to set a task for the whole group: make a big picture together. All participants work together here, each using their own rope.

Possible errors:
The rope is stuck in between the big toe and the toe next to it. All toes are to be clawed.

Tip:
This is also a balance exercise. Clawing the toes enhances the plantar arch.

Exercise 2: **Marble Transport**

- ■ **Aim:** Strengthening of the toe bending muscles and the feet
- ■ **Type:** 2a: exercise by oneself, 2b: group exercise
- ■ **Equipment:** Marbles; ropes (1 rope per participant) or cardboard box

Starting position:
Standing with a rope (or box) and marbles in front of everyone.

Procedure:
2a: The rope must be shaped into a closed form, so that the marbles don't roll away (e.g. a circle or a square). The rope or the box is then placed further away, depending on the children's age and skills. Without using their hands, the children must transport the marbles to the target. Just how the children do this is up to them; some will probably hop along; others will walk on their heels.

2b: Exercise 2a should definitely be done beforehand for practice. For the group exercise, or in order to make things more tricky, the rope or box is placed in the middle, and the participants form a circle all the same distance away from the center.
As all children and participants have the same number of marbles, the idea is to transport all the marbles to the middle as quickly as possible. The children can decide themselves how many marbles they can take at a time.

Possible errors:
The marbles should not be placed on the foot, but should be in the toes' claws.

Tip:
Exercising in an upright position is also good balance training.

Exercise 3: Caterpillar

- ◼ **Aim:** Strengthening of the foot and toe flexing muscles
- ◼ **Type:** Individual exercise
- ◼ **Equipment:** None

Starting position:
Supine position with knees up.

Procedure:
Arms are lying relaxed beside the body, and the bottom is raised, so that the body forms a line. This position is kept up during the caterpillar walk. With all toes in claw position, the legs push themselves forward a few centimeters. The position of the trunk should be kept up, and for this reason, the caterpillar walk should take the reverse direction after a brief walk.

Possible errors:
One must make sure that the bottom does not sag during the exercise.

Tip:
Due to the starting position, this exercise also strengthens trunk muscles, hip-stretching posterior muscles, and the muscles of the rear thigh.

Exercise 4: **Flycatching Frogs**

- **Aim:** Strengthening of the lower leg muscles
- **Type:** Individual exercise
- **Equipment:** None

Starting position:
Crouching position on the floor with the hands on the floor between both legs; knees are pointing outwards.

Procedure:
Now every child has to jump forward like a frog, and catch flies in mid-flight by clapping their hands. A task could be, for example, try and catch ten flies.

Possible errors:
Children often try to make the exercise easier by not going back completely into the crouched position.

Tip:
As this exercise is made up of two tasks (jumping up and clapping), it also promotes children's coordinative skills. Not only are the muscles of the lower leg strengthened here, but all leg muscles.

Exercise 5: **Bird on One Leg**

- ■ **Aim:** Strengthening of the the calf muscles
- ■ **Type:** Individual exercise
- ■ **Equipment:** None

Starting position:
Standing at the wall with support.

Procedure:
One leg is raised; the other leg comes into tiptoe position, and then goes back down again. The instructor counts out loud, thus determining the tempo at the same time.

Possible errors:
The toestand is not carried out completely; the heels are only lifted to a minimal extent.

Exercise **6:** **Sawing Exercise**

■ **Aim:** Strengthening of the foot and lower leg muscles
■ **Type:** With a partner
■ **Equipment:** A rope for each pair

Starting position:
Kneeling position on one leg, slightly apart from each other.

Procedure:
The rope is knotted at both ends, and each participant grasps the rope with both hands. The upper body is moved back and forth in alternation, thus activating the foot and lower leg muscles. This occurs through the weight shift, i.e. the forward bending of the upper body.

Possible errors:
One should make sure that the weight is not only on the back leg, but that the foot at the front is pressed to the floor.

Tip:
The starting position demands good balance skills. In addition, when the exercise is carried out correctly, the hip flexing muscles of the back leg are stretched.

Exercise 7: **Windscreen Wipers**

- ■ **Aim:** Strengthening of the lower leg muscles
- ■ **Type:** Exercise with a partner
- ■ **Equipment:** None

Starting position:
Sitting position, opposite each other with legs stretched out in front, soles touching.

Procedure:
Now the windscreen wipers are turned on, and each pair has to move his feet left and right like wipers. The 6-8year-olds can also steer with their arms, and make car sounds. In order to attain a strengthening effect, one should support oneself by placing the arms on the floor, and now continue the movement working against the resistance of the partner.

Possible errors:
Only the amount of resistance necessary to keep the movement flowing should be given when strengthening.

Tip:
Working against resistance in this exercise can be recommended for children of age 8 and upwards.

STRETCHING EXERCISES

Exercise 8: **Cross Your Feet**

■ **Aim:** Stretching of the shin muscles and toe-stretching muscles
■ **Type:** Individual exercise
■ **Equipment:** None

Starting position:
In upright position, the foot that is to be stretched is crossed over the supporting leg; the upper side of the toes are pressed into the floor.

Procedure:
Stretching occurs through a slight bending of the knee that is in an upright position. The instep is pushed forward until a stretching sensation can be felt on the arch of the foot and shin.

Possible errors:
It is possible for the foot to be in the right position without the instep being pushed forward.

Exercise **9:**   **Wall Support**

■ **Aim:**   Stretching of the calf muscles and Achilles tendon
■ **Type:**   Individual exercise
■ **Equipment:** None

Starting position:
Stride position in front of a wall. Both feet are pointing forward, and the hands are supporting the body at the wall.

Procedure:
Stretching takes place through the front leg bending, and taking on much more body weight; whereas, the back leg must remain fully stretched; the heel must not lift off the floor.

Possible errors:
The rear heel frequently rises from the floor, or the rear knee does not stay outstretched. One must pay attention to the lumbar spine, as in many cases, there is strong evidence of lordosis here.

Exercise 10: **Push up Stretching**

- **Aim:** Stretching of the calf muscles and Achilles tendon
- **Type:** Individual exercise
- **Equipment:** None

Starting position:
One starts out in the push up position; both knees are slightly bent.

Procedure:
One leg is outstretched, and the heel is pushed toward the floor.

Possible errors:
The push up position is taxing to start off with; the spine can quickly end up curving. Marked evidence of lordosis in the lumbar area is also possible.

Tip:
The trunk is also strengthened.

Exercise 11: **Partner Support**

- ■ **Aim:** Stretching of the calf muscles and Achilles tendon
- ■ **Type:** Partner exercise
- ■ **Equipment:** None

Starting position:
Standing opposite each other in wide stride position; both feet are pointing forwards. The palms of the hands are flat, and touching those of the partner; the elbows are slightly bent and pointing outwards.

Procedure:
Stretching occurs through the front leg bending, and taking on much more body weight. The rear knee joint should stay stretched, and the heel must not come away from the floor. The partners can support each other in this position.

Possible errors:
The knee at the back is often unconsciously bent, or the heel is raised from the floor. One must always pay attention to the correct position of the lumbar spine here, as in many cases, there is strong evidence of lordosis.

Exercise 12: **Children of Stone**

- ■ **Aim:** Stretching of the calf muscles and rear thigh muscles
- ■ **Type:** Group exercise
- ■ **Equipment:** None

Procedure:
All children and adolescents go around the room. The sports instructor claps his hands, and all participants are "turned to stone" by placing their hands on the floor in front of them, keeping their knees stretched. The hands are a distance away from the feet so that the heels are still touching the floor. Then, the teacher taps one participant on the back, and this child must begin to free the rest of the group. He does this by crawling or wriggling under another child's stomach. This newly "released" child also starts helping to free the other "stone" children until at the end all children have been released.

Possible errors:
One must ensure that the knees don't bend, or that the heels don't lift up.

Tip:
This playful form of stretching is particularly good for children between 6 and 8 years of age.

7.2 Strengthening and Stretching Leg and Hip Muscles

STRENGTHENING EXERCISES

Exercise 13: Wall Sliding

- **Aim:** Strengthening of the front thigh muscles
- **Type:** Individual exercise.
- **Equipment:** None

Starting position:
Standing with the back to the wall, feet are a slight distance away from the wall.

Procedure:
One slides down the wall with the back straight until the knees form a maximum angle of 90°. The knees should be pointing slightly outwards, and the feet should be wider apart from each other than the hips. Every participant has to hang out in this end position for several seconds.

Possible errors:
Knees point inwards, or the shoulder blades come away from the wall.

Tip:
A more difficult version for the group is to raise the heels a number of times in this end position.

Exercise 16: **Stuck Together**

- **Aim:** Strengthening of the front thigh muscles
- **Type:** Partner exercise
- **Equipment:** None

Starting position:
The partners stand back-to-back.

Procedure:
By slowly bending the knees, the thigh muscles are strengthened, whereby both partners are supporting, or touching each other the whole time. A maximum angle of 90° should be attained, and the movement should be flowing without having to grind one's teeth in the end position.

Possible errors:
The knees point inwards as the partners move away each other.

Tip:
The sense of balance is also being worked on here.

Exercise **17: Target Throwing:**

- ■ **Aim:** Strengthening of the front thigh muscles
- ■ **Type:** Partner exercise
- ■ **Equipment:** 1 ball per pair

Starting position:
The partners stand in stride position opposite each other, several paces apart. The entire body weight is on the front leg, which is also bent at the knee. To aid balance somewhat, the leg behind should only be touching the floor with the tiptoes.

Procedure:
This position should be kept while the ball is passed to each other. Many variations are possible; here are a few examples:
* Throw the ball with one or both hands.
* Get the ball to bounce in the middle.
* Throw the ball with both hands above head height.
* Let the ball circle the body once before being passed back again.
* Let the ball swing a few times alongside the body before being passed to the partner etc.

Possible errors:
This exercise is hard to carry out when the children or adolescents are not capable of aiming properly. For this reason, one should not set difficult tasks with the ball. Another mistake is when the body weight is on both legs.

Tip:
This exercise offers a strengthening effect, and is also good balance training.

Exercise 18: **Trees in the Wind**

- ■ **Aim:** Strengthening of the front thigh muscles
- ■ **Type:** Group exercise
- ■ **Equipment:** None

Starting position:
The group is in a circle kneeling, but leaning back on their heels. The arms are stretched down alongside the body, but the hands are pointing to the front.

Procedure:
Now all participants must tense their abdominal muscles, and come into an upright kneeling position. The body forms a line; the arms press down toward the floor like roots. The group is divided into two sub-groups, and now one group can make wind sounds as the trees sway to and fro, the weight being shifted forward and backward.

Possible errors:
When shifting body weight, the body must be as stiff as a tree; otherwise, the posterior falls back, and no tension of the thigh muscles occurs.

Tip:
Trunk and posterior muscles are also strengthened here.

Exercise **19**: **Tightening the Rope**

- ■ **Aim:** Strengthening of the abductors (outer thigh muscles)
- ■ **Type:** Individual exercise
- ■ **Equipment:** Ropes (one rope per participant)

Starting position:
Lateral position, each child or adolescent has tied a knot in his rope, and places his feet in the loop.

Procedure:
Strengthening occurs through the upper leg being lifted in stretched position until the rope is under tension. One must make sure that the toes are pointing forwards, and not upward. The strengthening effect can be intensified by keeping the leg raised in the air for several seconds.

Possible errors:
The upper side of the pelvis often falls back unconsciously.

Tip:
There are numerous variations possible here using this starting position, e.g. circling the upper leg in the air, bicycle.

Exercise 20: Holding the Ball

- ■ **Aim:** Strengthening of the "hip stretching" (posterior) muscles
- ■ **Type:** Individual exercise
- ■ **Equipment:** Gymnastic balls (one ball per participant)

Starting position:
Supine position with knees bent. The gymnastic ball is placed between the knees, and held there by the legs.

Procedure:
The arms are then stretched out behind the head, the posterior is raised until the entire trunk forms a straight line.

20a: Two variations are possible here, and they can be carried out after each other. In the first variation, the trunk remains in the stable bridge position; the feet roll onto the toes and heels in alternation without the ball being lost.

20b: The trunk remains in bridge position with the ball between the knees as above, but this time, each leg is outstretched in turn and in line with the trunk.

Possible errors:
The posterior must not sag.

Tip:
The trunk muscles and knees are also strengthened here.

Exercise 21: **Walking the Dog**

- ■ **Aim:** Strengthening of the abductors (outer thigh muscles) and posterior muscles
- ■ **Type:** Partner exercise
- ■ **Equipment:** One rope per pair

Starting position:
One child is a dog and on all fours, the second child a dog-owner who wants to take him for a walk. The rope is wrapped loosely around the dog's stomach, and this lead is held loosely by the owner.

Procedure:
All pairs can walk around the room, and the dogs then cock their leg, i.e. bend and lift one leg out to the side, and hold it there for several seconds.

Possible errors:
One keeps using the same leg.

Tip:
The instructor must remind the participants to switch roles.

Exercise 22: Leg Presses

■ **Aim:** Strengthening of the abductors and adductors (inner and outer thigh muscles)
■ **Type:** Partner exercise
■ **Equipment:** None

Starting position:
Both partners sit opposite each other with their legs outstretched, and support themselves on their lower arms.

Procedure:
The outer side of one child's foot presses against the inside of the partner's foot. He in turn must press inward to build up resistance.

Possible errors:
One must make sure that the knees are neither turned inwards nor outwards.

> **Tip:**
This exercise is also possible when the legs are bent; resistance is then given by the knees.

Exercise **23**: **Ball Squashing**

- ■ **Aim:** Strengthening of the adductors, the inner thigh muscles
- ■ **Type:** Individual exercise
- ■ **Equipment:** A gymnastic or pezzi ball per person

Starting position:
In supine position, the slightly bent legs lift the ball, and hold it there.

Procedure:
Strengthening occurs through an even "squashing" of the ball for several seconds.

Possible errors:
At the end of the exercise, the ball should be lowered again slowly, and under tension, and not just dropped onto the floor.

Tip:
It's important that the size of the ball is more or less appropriate for the height of the child. This varies from a diameter of 35cm for kindergarten age, up to 45 cm, 55 cm, and 65 cm for a person of up to 175cm.

Exercise 24: **Skipping Rope in Many Variations**

■ **Aim:** Strengthening of the entire leg muscles
■ **Type:** Individual exercise
■ **Equipment:** One rope per person

Procedure:
Each participant receives a rope. It's a good idea to begin with easy tasks, such as:
* Forward skipping with and without hops in between
* Leg changing while skipping

More tricky:
* Crossing over of the rope while skipping
* Skipping on one leg
* Skipping, running forwards and backwards with the rope
* Crossing over the rope while running

Possible errors:
Skipping often becomes more difficult because the rope is too short or too long. To prevent this, one should stand on the rope, and adjust the length to shoulder height.

Tip:
Rope skipping is also very good for improving coordination.

Exercise **25: Snake Hunting**

■ **Aim:** Strengthening of the entire leg muscles
■ **Type:** Group exercise
■ **Equipment:** Several ropes

Starting position:
Depending on the size of the group, groups of four, five and six are formed, each with one or two "snake hunters" in the middle of the circle.

Procedure:
The kids, big kids or teens wriggle the ropes across the floor, while the snake hunter in the middle tries to jump onto a rope. When a "snake" has been captured, the roles are switched.

Possible errors:
One must make sure that the ropes do actually touch the floor when being wriggled.

Tip:
This exercise promotes children's skills of reaction.

STRETCHING EXERCISES

Exercise 26: Flick Knife

■ **Aim:** Stretching of the front thigh muscles
■ **Type:** Individual exercise
■ **Equipment:** None

Starting position:
Prone position.

Procedure:
The right leg is stretched when the right hand takes hold of that ankle, and pulls the heel up to the posterior.

Possible errors:
The leg that is to be stretched is to be kept parallel to the other leg; one often unconsciously moves it out to the side. The spinal column must not end up in a sideward position.

Tip:
If there is too much evidence of lordosis in the lumbar area, one can alleviate this by tucking a cushion under the stomach.

Exercise 27: Kneeling Position at the Wall

■ **Aim:** Stretching of the front thigh muscles
■ **Type:** Individual exercise
■ **Equipment:** None

Starting position:
The group is dispersed around the room, so that every participant has a place at the wall. One takes a lunge step, and then goes into a genuflecting position.

Procedure:
The foot at the back is grasped by that hand, and pulled toward the posterior; the weight is shifted to the front while the other hand holds onto the wall.

Possible errors:
One must pay attention to the position of the lumbar spine.

Exercise 28: Who Can Stay Standing on One Leg for the Longest?

■ **Aim:** Stretching of the front thigh muscles
■ **Type:** Individual exercise
■ **Equipment:** None

Starting position:
Upright position.

Procedure:
The right foot is grasped by that hand, and pulled toward the posterior. The other arm is used for balancing.

Possible errors:
One must make sure that the leg to be stretched does not drift out to the side; an overstretching of the lumbar spine must also be avoided.

Tip:
This exercise can also be carried out at the wall.

Exercise **29: Circling the Body**

- ■ **Aim:**   Stretching of the rear thigh muscles
- ■ **Type:**   Individual exercise
- ■ **Equipment:** Gymnastic ball, one ball per person

Starting position:
Straddled sitting position, the spine is upright.

Procedure:
The ball is rolled around the first foot, and then the second foot, as well as behind the back.

Possible errors:
Bending of the knees.

Tip:
The back muscles and inner thigh muscles are also stretched in this exercise.

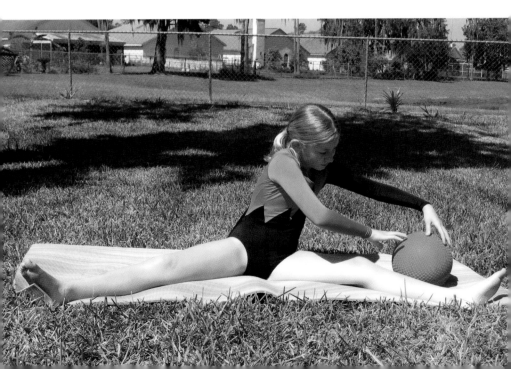

Exercise **30**: **Press the Ball Against the Wall**

- **Aim:** Stretching of the rear thigh muscles
- **Type:** Individual exercise
- **Equipment:** Gymnastic ball, one per person

Starting position:
Sitting facing the wall with legs outstretched.

Procedure:
The arms are stretched out to the front at shoulder height. The task here is to try to press the ball against the wall while keeping your back straight.

Possible errors:
Bending of the knees.

Exercise **31: Leg Up**

- ▪ **Aim:** Stretching of the rear thigh muscles
- ▪ **Type:** Individual exercise
- ▪ **Equipment:** Wall bars or box

Starting position:
Standing facing wall bars or box.

Procedure:
One leg is placed on the box or bar; the pelvis remains straight, and the other leg is fully stretched. Stretching of the thigh muscles occurs by leaning the upper body toward the high leg, slowly and in an upright position.

Possible errors:
The leg to be stretched is often placed up too high.

Tip:
One should start the stretching exercises using the lower bars, and then gradually move up.

Exercise 34: **Partner Roll**

- **Aim:** Stretching of the hip flexing muscles
- **Type:** Partner exercise
- **Equipment:** One pezzi ball per pair

Starting position:
Kneeling position in front of the ball.

Procedure:
Partner A lays one leg onto the ball, and partner B assists here by holding A's hands at the front. A continues pushing himself on until his front foot is on the floor and the hip flexing muscles of the rear leg are stretched. The leg to be stretched only touches the floor with the toes.

Possible errors:
Rounding of the spinal column.

Tip:
The pushing movement can be practiced in an earlier exercise without the front foot touching the floor. This exercise demands a very good sense of balance.

Exercise **35: Tall Arches**

- **Aim:** Stretching of the hip flexing muscles
- **Type:** Group exercise
- **Equipment:** Two gymnastic balls

Starting position:
Two rows are formed, standing opposite each other.

Procedure:
All children and adolescents place their right foot forward, thus shifting body weight to the front. The knee forms a maximum angle of 90°; the rear leg is stretched. This stretched position must be held for several seconds as the first child in each row rolls the gymnastic ball through the arch on his side, i.e. under the other children's legs. When the ball has arrived at the other end, the last child in each row takes the ball, runs to the front, and lets it roll through the arch again.

Possible errors:
The rear knee touches the floor.

Tip:
A changeover of legs can take place after every second roll of the ball, depending on how fast the group is.

Exercise **36: Butterfly**

- ■ **Aim:**   Stretching of the adductors (inner thigh muscles)
- ■ **Type:**   Individual exercise
- ■ **Equipment:** None

Starting position:
Cross-legged sitting position, soles of the feet are touching and the knees fall to the side.

Procedure:
The feet are drawn in close to the body; the elbows slowly press the knees down towards the floor.

Possible errors:
The trunk must stay in an upright position.

Tip:
The sports instructor can call out tasks, e.g. open your wings slowly and close them again.

Exercise **37**: **Ants on Your Legs**

- ▪ **Aim:**   Stretching of the adductors (inner thigh muscles)
- ▪ **Type:**   Individual exercise
- ▪ **Equipment:** None

Starting position:
Sitting with legs outstretched and straddled.

Procedure:
With the upper body in upright position, the fingers start crawling like ants over the legs from the thighs to the ankles, and then back up again.

Possible errors:
The upper body is extremely bent.

Tip:
Carrying this exercise out slowly results in a better stretching effect.

Exercise **38: Right and Left**

- ■ **Aim:** Stretching of the adductors (inner thigh muscles)
- ■ **Type:** Partner exercise
- ■ **Equipment:** None

Starting position:
The partners stand opposite each other in wide straddled position, and the feet are pointing to the front.

Procedure:
Both partners simultaneously shift their body weight onto their right leg, which is then in a strong bent position. At the same time, the left leg is being stretched. After several seconds, the weight is shifted again simultaneously to the left leg.

Possible errors:
The sports trainer must always ensure that the participants do not turn their body sideways, but stay upright all the time.

Tip:
It is also possible to rest one's arms on the bent leg.

Exercise **39**: **Rainbow**

- ■ **Aim:** Stretching of the adductors
- ■ **Type:** Individual exercise
- ■ **Equipment:** None

Starting position:
Supine position at a wall, the posterior is right up at the wall and the legs are leaning against the wall in a stretched position.

Procedure:
The legs fall out to the side, their own weight causing the stretching effect.

Possible errors:
The posterior is too far away from the wall.

Tip:
With a kids group, it is possible to hide the "rainbow" by pulling the legs toward the body. The "rainbow" appears again when the stretching is repeated.

Exercise **40**: **Revolving Seat:**

- ■ **Aim:** Stretching of the abductors (outer thigh muscles)
- ■ **Type:** Individual exercise
- ■ **Equipment:** None

Starting position:
Sitting position with legs out straight, the leg to be stretched is bent and crosses the other leg at knee height.

Procedure:
The left leg is stretched when the upper body turns to the right; the left upper arm pushes the right leg away to the left.

Possible errors:
No stretching takes place when the bent leg is not pushed over properly to the other side.

Tip:
The trunk muscles are also stretched in this exercise.

Exercise 41: Hands of the Clock

- ◼ **Aim:** Stretching of the abductors (outer thigh muscles)
- ◼ **Type:** Individual exercise
- ◼ **Equipment:** None

Starting position:
Supine position.

Procedure:
The leg to be stretched lifts straight up into the air slowly, and is then lowered, and placed down on the other side. The pelvis is also turned in this exercise.

Possible errors:
Shoulders should stay on the floor.

Tip:
This exercise can be made more intresting for kids and big kids when one calls out the time, e.g. 3 o'clock, 4 o'clock.

Exercise 42: Leg to the Stomach

■ **Aim:**   Stretching of the hip stretching (posterior) muscles
■ **Type:**   Individual exercise
■ **Equipment:** None

Starting position:
Supine position.

Procedure:
One leg is pulled as near as possible toward the body. The other leg must remain stretched and pressed into the floor.

Possible errors:
One must make sure that the outstretched leg does not bend. The participants are not to pull at their leg for all they're worth, but must stay in supine position.

Exercise **43: Leg Up and Out to the Side**

■ **Aim:**   Stretching of the hip-stretching and other posterior
                  muscles
■ **Type:**   Individual exercise
■ **Equipment:** None

Starting position:
Supine position with knees up; one leg is crossed over the other.

Procedure:
The leg to be stretched is pulled towards the body, and at the same time,
out over to the other side.

Possible errors:
The pelvis does not stay entirely on the floor.

Exercise **46**: **Roll the Ball**

- ■ **Aim:**   Strengthening of the back muscles
- ■ **Type:**   Individual exercise
- ■ **Equipment:** Pezzi balls, one ball per person

Starting position:
Supine position with the lower legs leaning on the ball. The arms are lying on the floor alongside the body for balance.

Procedure:
The posterior is raised until the trunk and thighs form a straight line. By bending the knees, the ball is then rolled as near to the body as possible. The legs are stretched again slowly after this.

Possible errors:
The posterior is not lifted up properly.

Tip:
This exercise also strengthens posterior muscles, and the rear thigh muscles.

Exercise **47: Creeping Dog**

- ■ **Aim:** Strengthening of the back muscles
- ■ **Type:** Group exercise
- ■ **Equipment:** None

Starting position:
All participants are on all fours, in a line, waiting to cross the room.

Procedure:
The participants prop themselves up on their toes. They start creeping by lifting their knees up from the floor to a minimal extent, and then walking on tiptoes.

Possible errors:
It's very important to remind the group to only barely lift up their knees.

Tip:
In a group of 6-8 year-olds, it's a good idea to lay a sack of sand on their backs to stop them from lifting up their knees too much.

Exercise **48**: **Who Has no Balloons?**

■ **Aim:** Strengthening of the back muscles
■ **Type:** Group exercise
■ **Equipment:** Balloons

Starting position:
The participants are in two rows facing each other, and only separated from each other by a line. They are sitting on the floor with their knees up, and they are supported by their arms at the back which are fully stretched.

Procedure:
The posterior is raised, so that the upper body and thighs are the same height. The sports instructor throws the same amount of balloons into both fields. Both groups now try to get as many balloons as possible out of their field. The players transport the balloons to the other side of the field by using their feet only.

Possible errors:
The posterior sags.

Tip:
The balloons which have left the playing area are deposited again into the right field by the trainer or a helper. This game lasts for 1-2 minutes, depending on performance level.

Exercise **49**: **Trot**

- ■ **Aim:**   Strengthening of the back muscles
- ■ **Type:**   Individual exercise
- ■ **Equipment:** None

Starting position:
On all fours (quadruped position).

Procedure:
At the beginning, every participant should try to lift the diagonal extremities to a minimum extent. If no problems arise doing this, it is then possible to go on to the faster variation (trot).

Possible errors:
In quadruped position the hands must always be under the shoulder joints, and the knees under the hips.

Tip:
Working with the diagonals is a form of coordination training.

Exercise **50: Rubberband**

- ■ **Aim:** Strengthening of the back muscles
- ■ **Type:** Individual exercise
- ■ **Equipment:** None

Starting position:
Quadruped position.

Procedure:
One starts working on the diagonal extremities, for instance the elbow touches the opposite knee, both limbs are then outstretched, and stay in this position for few seconds. These movements should be similar to a rubber band which is slowly being pulled tight.

Possible errors:
Arms and legs are not fully stretched.

Tip:
Exercise 49 is good practice for this exercise.

Exercise **51: Flying Balloons**

- ■ **Aim:**   Strengthening of the stomach muscles
- ■ **Type:**   Group exercise
- ■ **Equipment:** Balloons

Starting position:
The group forms a circle, and all participants lie down on their backs with their heads in the middle of the circle.

Procedure:
The participants put their knees up and stretch the arms up into the air. The trainer throws a few balloons in and each participant must try to keep the balloons up in the air by lifting his head and shoulders, and hitting the balloons with his hands.

Possible errors:
Hitting the balloons without raising one's head and shoulders.

Exercise 52: Bike Tour

- ■ **Aim:**   Strengthening of the vertical abdominal muscles
- ■ **Type:**   Partner exercise
- ■ **Equipment:** None

Starting position:
Supine position with feet touching.

Procedure:
The soles of the feet press against each other; the legs are lifted at the same time. The participants then raise their head from the mat while the arms are akimbo, facing the feet. The instructor starts the tour by indicating the tempo (e.g. uphill, downhill or in rocking position), and whether forwards or backwards. A few breaks are needed here.

Possible errors:
As soon as the arm and head positions are no longer accurate, there is strong evidence of lordosis in the lumbar spinal area.

Tip:
The "bike tour" also strengthens all leg muscles.

Exercise 53: Show Me Your Hands

- **Aim:** Strengthening of the oblique abdominal muscles
- **Type:** Individual exercise
- **Equipment:** None

Starting position:
The partners are lying in supine position opposite each other; the legs form a 90° angle in the air, the soles of the feet are touching.

Procedure:
The arms remain stretched for the entire exercise. Each participant lifts their head, and one shoulder towards his feet. He stretches both his arms to the side, so that he is able to see his partner's hands.

Possible errors:
Head and shoulder remain on the floor.

Tip:
This is often a lot of fun with kids when they're holding something small in their hand at the same time, e.g. a little ball or furry toy.

Exercise 54: **Beetle on His Back**

- ■ **Aim:**   Strengthening of the abdominal muscles
- ■ **Type:**   Individual exercise
- ■ **Equipment:** None

Starting position:
Supine position with arms stretched upwards.

Procedure:
One elbow touches the opposite knee, and stretches out again on the floor before the same movement begins with the other diagonal.

Possible errors:
The exercise should not be carried out quickly as this hinders an effective tensing of the abdominal muscles.

Exercise **55: Throwing the Ball**

■ **Aim:**   Strengthening of the vertical abdominal muscles
■ **Type:**   Partner exercise
■ **Equipment:** One gymnastic ball per pair

Starting position:
Supine straddled position with the knees up. The partner is in upright position not far away.

Procedure:
The person standing throws the ball carefully to his partner lying down who in turn has to catch the ball, and throw it back by lifting his head and shoulders.

Possible errors:
The lumbar spine also lifts up.

Tip:
This exercise can also be done with adolescents using a medicine ball.

Exercise **56: Runway**

- ■ **Aim:** Strengthening of the abdominal and posterior muscles
- ■ **Type:** Partner exercise
- ■ **Equipment:** Gymnastic balls (one ball per pair)

Starting position:
Supine position supported on lower arms.

Procedure:
The legs are stretched out beside each other on the floor. The shoulderblades are pulled together, the posterior is lifted up until the body forms a straight line. This position must be held while the partner rolls the ball from the chest down to the feet several times. A little rolling tournament is possible here. The group who manages to roll the ball most frequently are the winners.

Possible errors:
Sagging of the posterior.

Tip:
This exercise also strengthens the shoulder muscles.

STRENGTHENING EXERCISES FOR THE TRUNK

Exercise 57: **Man in the Moon**

- ■ **Aim:** Stretching of the lateral back and abdominal muscles
- ■ **Type:** Individual exercise
- ■ **Equipment:** Batons (one baton per person)

Starting position:
Supine position with baton in the hands, the baton is placed down on the floor above the head.

Procedure:
Both legs wander to one side with little steps without the pelvis lifting from the floor. Having attained the maximal degree of movement, one now lets the arms wander to this side still holding the baton. A moon shape is clearly visible.

Possible errors:
Raising of the pelvis or the shoulders.

Tip:
Remain in the end position for a while before stretching the other side.

Exercise 58: Tightening the Bow

■ **Aim:**   Stretching of the back muscles and lateral abdominal
            muscles
■ **Type:**   Individual exercises
■ **Equipment:** None

Starting position:
Upright position when the right side is to be stretched then the right leg
should be crossed over.

Procedure:
The right arm is stretched upwards, and then pulled up towards the
ceiling, leaning minimally towards the other side.

Possible errors:
The trunk must stay in
an upright position. It
must neither bend nor
end up in a hollow
position.

Tip:
A variation of this
stretching exercise is
when both arms are in
the air holding a baton
in the hands.

Exercise 59: Stretching in Pairs

- ■ **Aim:** Stretching of the back and abdominal muscles
- ■ **Type:** Partner exercise
- ■ **Equipment:** None

Starting position:
The partners are in a supine position with their arms stretched out behind them grasping each other's hands.

Procedure:
The participants put one knee up, and place this foot on the outer side of the other knee. Now they must try to touch the floor on the other side with this knee.

Possible errors:
Raising of the shoulders.

Tip:
The pectoral and shoulder areas are also stretched.

Exercise **60:** **Sitting Cross-legged**

- **Aim:** Stretching of the back muscles
- **Type:** Individual exercise
- **Equipment:** None

Starting position:
Sitting cross legged.

Procedure:
In this exercise, one must try to crawl forward with one's hands as far as possible, and then to the side.

Possible errors:
The posterior must remain on the floor.

Tip:
The pectoral and shoulder areas are also stretched.

Exercise **61**: **Parcel**

- ■ **Aim:** Stretching of the back muscles
- ■ **Type:** Partner exercise
- ■ **Equipment:** Ropes

Starting position:
Supine position.

Procedure:
One child is the parcel, and his partner the post office official. The "parcel"is lying on his back, and pulls his legs in towards his trunk as far as possible, and tucks in his head. The official can now tie the ropes loosely around his arms and legs. The parcel must not move, but stay in this position for several seconds.

Warning!
Only tie the rope around arms and legs, and nowhere near the head!

Tip:
One can do this exercise without the ropes for adolescents.

Exercise 62: Trunk Twisting

- **Aim:** Stretching of the back and abdominal muscles
- **Type:** Partner exercise
- **Equipment:** Gymnastic balls (one ball per pair)

Starting position:
Kneeling position, leaning back on the heels, almost back to back.

Procedure:
By turning the trunk to the side, and with the arms stretched, one passes the ball to one's partner.

Possible errors:
The group must be constantly reminded to keep the upper body upright as the turning movement is hindered otherwise.

Tip:
The ball should be passed slowly, and not in a jerky movement.

Exercise **63**: **Snake**

- ■ **Aim:** Stretching of the vertical abdominal muscles
- ■ **Type:** Individual exercise
- ■ **Equipment:** None

Starting position:
Prone position.

Procedure:
a) One props oneself up onto one's lower arms slowly, so that the spinal column is stretched properly.
b) To intensify this, it is also possible to support oneself on one's hands, and one stays in this position for several seconds. The elbows must not be completely straightened here, only minimally bent.

Possible errors:
The head must not be overstretched, but always be an extension of the spine in this exercise.

Tip:
When doing this exercise with kids, one can also introduce snake noises.

9 EXERCISES FOR STRENGTHENING AND STRETCHING THE UPPER EXTREMITIES

STRENGTHENING OF THE UPPER EXTREMITIES

Exercise **64: Matching Strength**

- ■ **Aim:** Strengthening of the shoulder and pectoral muscles
- ■ **Type:** Partner exercise
- ■ **Equipment:** None

Starting position:
Stride position opposite each other, elbows at 90° and pointing outwards, hands are together. One partner holds both his hands out towards his partner, his hands are pressed together lightly. The other partner does the same with his hands, and they end up outside his partner's hands.

Procedure:
The partner with his hands on the inside pushes his hands outwards against his partner, who is pushing his hands inwards, and also strengthening his pectoral muscles.

Possible errors:
One often forgets to lift the elbows up out to the side.

Tip:
Particularly suitable for a group of teens.

Exercise 65: Wheelbarrow Race

■ **Aim:**   Strengthening of the shoulder and arm muscles
■ **Type:**   Group exercise
■ **Equipment:** None

Starting position:
The group is divided into four teams who all get into a row in pairs behind each other. One partner starts off in an upright position; the other partner, i.e. the wheelbarrow, in quadruped position.

Procedure:
It is important that the running partner grasps the "wheelbarrow's" thighs so that his legs are on either side of him. The sports trainer gives a start signal, and the race begins. When the participants arrive at one end, they then switch roles, and head off again.

Possible errors:
Holding the wheelbarrow by his ankles or calves puts too much strain on the spine.

Tip:
One can use bigger or smaller teams as preferred.

Exercise **66: Push ups on the Wall**

■ **Aim:**   Strengthening of the shoulder and arm muscles
■ **Type:**   Individual exercises
■ **Equipment:** None

Starting position:
Standing facing the wall, a large step away.

Procedure:
With tensed abdominal muscles and elbows out to the side, one leans towards the wall and pushes oneself back again by outstretching the arms. While the body moves forward, one should try and clap hands as often as possible.

Possible errors:
Overstretching of the spine.

Tip:
It is possible to carry out this exercise with teens using one arm only; the other arm is resting on that shoulder. The upper body should not be twisted, however.

Exercise **67**: **Bascule Bridge**

- ■ **Aim:** Strengthening of the shoulder and arm (elbow-stretching) muscles
- ■ **Type:** Individual exercise
- ■ **Equipment:** None

Starting position:
Participants are lying on the floor with their knees up, and are supported by their hands at the back. Fingers are pointing to the front.

Procedure:
A bridge is formed: the arms are stretched out and the trunk forms a horizontal line. The trunk must remain stable during the entire exercise whereas the elbows keep bending and stretching.

Possible errors:
It is very important to keep an eye on: the elbows must not be stretched to a maximum as children and adolescents in particular have joints which can be overstretched.

Exercise **68: Let the Ball Hop**

■ **Aim:** Strengthening of the arm and shoulder muscles
■ **Type:** Partner exercise
■ **Equipment:** One gymnastic ball and scarf or towel per pair

Starting position:
All pairs stand opposite each other, each holding one end of the scarf.

Procedure:
A ball is laid on the scarf, and the participants must try to get this ball up into the air as often as possible, and catch it again. With big kids and teens, it is possible to have more advanced variations of this, e.g. swapping places when the ball is in the air, or walking around the room throughout the exercise.

Tip:
To get kids used to this exercise, it's a good idea to start off by rolling the ball to and fro.

Exercise **69**: **Swinging Scarves**

- ■ **Aim:**   Strengthening of the arm and shoulder muscles
- ■ **Type:**   Group exercise
- ■ **Equipment:** One scarf per person

Starting position:
Standing in a circle.

Procedure:
Each participant should try to perform an exercise with the scarf e.g. waving the scarf above one's head, spinning it beside one's body, figure eights, semi-circles, drawing snakes in the air with one or both hands etc.

Tip:
When doing this exercise with kids, it's a good idea to call out some playful or practical examples, such as cleaning windows, cleaning the car, waving goodbye etc. There is no limit to one's imagination here.

Exercise 70: **Locomotive**

- **Aim:** Strengthening of the arm and shoulder muscles
- **Type:** Partner exercise
- **Equipment:** Two batons per pair

Starting position:
The pair are standing behind each other, both facing the same direction.

Procedure:
Both partners stretch their arms, and take hold of the baton at each end, and move the arms up and down alternately – like a locomotive – and walk around the room. The person at the back should brake occasionally by offering resistance on the batons.

Possible errors:
Turning the trunk is not allowed as this hinders arm activity.

Tip:
Don't forget to change partners!
A teen group can also do this exercise facing each other.

STRETCHING OF THE UPPER EXTRMITIES

Exercise 71: Let Yourself Hang

- ■ **Aim:** Stretching of the pectoral and shoulder muscles
- ■ **Type:** Partner exercise
- ■ **Equipment:** One pezzi ball per pair

Starting position:
Quadruped position in front of the ball.

Procedure:
Stretching takes place when the arms are laid upon the ball, and the upper body is stretched and left hanging.

Possible errors:
Leaning the posterior back on the heels.

Tip:
It is also possible for three or four children to use one ball for stretching.

Exercise 72: **Thirsty Cat**

■ **Aim:**   Stretching of the pectoral and shoulder muscles
■ **Type:**   Individual exercise
■ **Equipment:** None

Starting position:
Quadruped position.

Procedure:
The arms drift out to the front as far as possible. The trunk is now stretched until the head is only a few centimeters above the floor. The kids group pretend to be cats taking a drink.

Possible errors:
Leaning the posterior back on the heels.

Tip:
In order to make this stretching exercise more amusing, one can ask the children some questions such as:
Does a cat drink mineral water, coke or orange juice? Does it drink milk or water?. Show me how a cat drinks, etc

Exercise **73: Stretching at the Wall**

- ■ **Aim:** Stretching of the pectoral muscles
- ■ **Type:** Individual exercise
- ■ **Equipment:** None

Starting position:
Stride position sideways to a wall.

Procedure:
The arm to be stretched is bent, and the lower arm leans against the wall. As the large pectoral muscle consists of many parts, it is stretched at two different heights. First of all, the arm is leaning against the wall with the elbow at ear height; then, the elbow forms a 90°. Once the arm is in position, one starts stretching by leaning the upper body forward, and shifting more weight onto the front leg.

Possible errors:
The lumbar spine must not be overstretched.

Tip:
This form of stretching can particularly be recommended for teens.

Exercise 74: Scratching Your Back

- **Aim:** Stretching of the upper arm (elbow-stretching) muscles
- **Type:** Individual exercise
- **Equipment:** None

Starting position:
Upright position.

Procedure:
The intended arm is stretched up in the air, and then flexed in such a way that the hand ends up between the shoulder blades. The other hand pulls the elbow downwards, allowing the fingers to crawl further down the back.

Possible errors:
The head must stay straight.

Tip:
Kids and big kids can scratch their backs during the stretching phase.

Exercise 75: Morning Flower

■ **Aim:**   Stretching of the shoulder and upper arm (elbow-stretching) muscles
■ **Type:**   Individual exercise
■ **Equipment:** None

Starting position:
The group is in a circle, kneeling and leaning back on their heels.

Procedure:
The upper body lies down to the front (parcel position), and the arms are folded behind the back. The instructor calls out when the flower is to open up slowly, and the group all raise their upper body up to 45°, and bring their stretched arms upwards at the same time.

Possible errors:
The arms should not be bent but completely stretched.

Tip:
Stretching is possible in various starting positions, e.g sitting down on a ball or standing up.

Exercise *76:* **Partner Stretching**

- ■ **Aim:** Stretching of the upper arm muscles
- ■ **Type:** Partner exercise
- ■ **Equipment:** None

Starting position:
Both partners stand back-to-back approximately one stride away from each other.

Procedure:
One partner stretches his arm out to the back, and lays his hand on his partner's shoulder blade. His fingers should be touching the spine. He then turns the upper body away from the arm, and stays in this position for several seconds.

Possible errors:
The hand loses contact with the partner's shoulder.

Tip:
This stretching can also be done at a wall or wall of bars.

Exercise 77: **Stretching on All Fours**

- ■ **Aim:** Stretching of the lower arm (hand-bending) muscles
- ■ **Type:** Individual exercise
- ■ **Equipment:** None

Starting position:
Quadruped position.

Procedure:
Hands are turned outwards, so that the fingers are pointing towards the feet. With stretched arms, one then slowly shifts one's weight to the back.

Possible errors:
Bending of the arms.

Exercise 78: Wandering Ball

- **Aim:** Stretching of the lower arm (hand bending) muscles
- **Type:** Individual exercise
- **Equipment:** Gymnastic balls, one ball per person

Starting position:
Upright position holding a ball.

Procedure:
The ball is held in front of one's stomach, the fingers are pointing to the floor, and the hands are exercising pressure on the ball. The lower arms are then raised.

Possible errors:
When the fingers are not pointing to the floor as much as possible.

Tip:
This can also be done without using a ball.

Exercise **79**: **Submarine**

■ **Aim:** Stretching of the lower arm and hand muscles
■ **Type:** Group exercise
■ **Equipment:** None

Starting position:
In upright position dispersed around the room.

Procedure:
All children pretend to be submarines by stretching their arms up beside their head, clenching their fists, and bending their wrists. The fists are beside each other, and are looking out to the front. The group has to sneak around the room quietly, moving up and down by bending the knees and straightening them again, and without touching any other "submarine". At the end, all submarines park in a corner of the room.

Possible errors:
No stretching occurs when the wrists are not bent.

Tip:
The thigh muscles are also being strengthened in this exercise.

10 EXERCISES FOR STRENGTHENING THE WHOLE BODY

Exercise 80: Feet Together

- **Aim:** Strengthening of the whole body
- **Type:** Partner exercise
- **Equipment:** None

Starting position:
Sitting with knees up and supported at the back by the arms which are stretched.

Procedure:
The posterior is raised until the upper body and thighs form a straight line. This position is held while both partners raise one foot, and touch each other's soles. One partner's leg is then stretched while the other partner's leg bends, and the feet stay touching the whole time.

Possible errors:
One must ensure that the posterior does not sag.

Tip:
This exercise is particularly recommendable for big kids and teens.

Exercise **81: Mini Push Ups**

- ■ **Aim:** Strengthening of the whole body
- ■ **Type:** Individual exercise
- ■ **Equipment:** None

Starting position:
Prone position propped up on one's arms and with the knees bent.

Procedure:
The participants do several push ups; the hands and knees are touching the floor. For easiness the feet can be held up crossed in the air.

Possible errors:
The abdominal muscles must be tensed so as to avoid stretching the lumbar spinal area excessively.

Exercise **82: Diagonal Stretching**

■ **Aim:**   Strengthening of the whole body
■ **Type:**   Individual exercise
■ **Equipment:** None

Starting position:
Prone position with the arms stretched out in front.

Procedure:
The heels are flexed and pulled backwards. The head and one arm are raised several centimeters from the floor, as well as the opposite leg. The raised extremities try to stretch the body out completely. The head is an extension of the spinal column; eyes keep looking at the floor.

Possible errors:
Exaggerated lifting of the extremities causes overstretching. So does looking to the front.

Exercise **83: Salamander**

- ■ **Aim:** Strengthening of the whole body
- ■ **Type:** Individual exercise
- ■ **Equipment:** None

Starting position:
Prone position leaning on lower arms.

Procedure:
One leans on the lower arms; the toes are touching the floor. The stomach is tensed and in the air. At the same time, one leg is raised and bent out to the side slowly. The trunk must be kept in a stable position here.

Possible errors:
Overstretching and sideward turning of the lumbar spinal area.

Tip:
This exercise must be carried out slowly, i.e. it should represent a salamander creeping slowly on the spot.

Exercise **84**: **Sideward Push Up**

- ■ **Aim:** Strengthening of the whole body
- ■ **Type:** Individual exercise
- ■ **Equipment:** None

Starting position:
Lying on the side supported by lower arm, legs are lying on each other.

Procedure:
The participant props himself up on the side, so that the entire body forms a straight line. The leg on top is now raised a number of times with pointed toes towards the front, and is then lowered again slowly.

Possible errors:
One must make sure that the posterior does not sag.

Tip:
Athletes with strong trunk muscles can lift up their arm in addition to their leg.

11 IDENTIFYING DISTURBANCES IN BALANCE

A person with no sense of balance – mental or physical – is doomed to fall.

Being able to hold one's balance is a basic motor experience which accompanies us through our whole lives. This involves balancing our body in every position, and with every movement, so as to keep our head upright and prevent us from falling.

What we have to do is keep our center of gravity in the body's vertical gravitational line. If our center of gravity drifts out of line, our balancing reactions are needed. This occurs e.g. when we raise or stretch an arm, shift our hips, or take a lunge step in order to increase our surface of support.

These important compensatory movements do not take place early enough when children have a weak sense of balance. Their perception is too slow.

Disturbances in balance can be seen during dynamic balance activities such as roller skating, ice-skating or skiing.

In a sports lesson, these disturbances are evident e.g. when children have problems jumping on a trampoline, balancing, doing exercises on the dynaboard, walking on stilts, as well as when walking quickly.

A typical visible symptom among children with disturbances in balance is a fine collection of bruises over the body.

In order to incorporate basic motor experiences into a functional gymnastics session, one can recommend the following exercises for improving balance.

As disturbances in balance appear frequently among children and adolescents, it is important to emphasise this aspect in a gymnastics session.

11.1 Exercises for Balance Training

Exercise 85: Gymnasts

■ **Aim:** Improvement of balance
■ **Type:** Partner exercise
■ **Equipment:** Two long benches, mats

Starting position:
The participants stand in a row in front of a long bench.

Procedure:

Variation A:
One child is the gymnast, the partner walks along beside the bench, and offers assistance where necessary. The gymnast stands on the bench, and bends the left knee, the right leg remains straight, and now swings back and forward alongside the bench. The right leg, is then set down on the bench again in front of the left leg, and this time the left leg is swung. This exercise is repeated until the child reaches the end of the bench.

Variation B:
Following variation A, one goes on to variation B with the second bench.

Beginning as above, swinging the right and left leg in alternation, the participant then takes a little jump, turning 180° in mid-air. This is followed by a backward swing, and another little jump. Swinging now continues in a forward direction.

Possible errors:
In order to lower the risk of accident to a minimum, one must make sure that the children do not start their exercises too soon after the person before them. Mats should be laid on the floor beside the benches.

Tip:
If certain children are afraid or have difficulties doing exercise A, they should then repeat this exercise again on the second bench and not go on to B.

Exercise 86: Partner Imitation

- ■ **Aim:** Improvement of balance
- ■ **Type:** Partner exercise
- ■ **Equipment:** Dynaboard (one per person)
  Gymnastic mats (one per pair)

In order to do this exercise, the participants must be able to stand on the dynaboard by themselves.

Starting position:
Both children stand opposite each other on the dynaboard with enough distance between them.

Procedure:
One child slowly begins to carry out movements which the partner has to copy without coming off the dynaboard, such as arm movements, bending the knees, standing on one leg, knee stand with one leg.

Possible errors:
It's not a good idea to do the exercises too quickly as each child must find his balance, and be able to keep it. As well as this, it is difficult to imitate one's partner when the movements are done too quickly.

Tip:
When working with this equipment, all children must be barefoot when doing the exercises, and a gymnastic mat must be lying under every dynaboard.

Exercise **87**: **Walking the Rope**

■ **Aim:** Improvement of balance
■ **Type:** Group exercise
■ **Equipment:** Several ropes

Starting position:
Upright position, several ropes are tied together on the floor.

Procedure:
The first task is every child must balance on the rope. One can stretch the arms out to the side for assistance. Several variations are possible here for making the exercise more tricky.
• Walking backwards
• Walking forwards and backwards on tiptoes.
• Touching the left foot with the right hand and vice versa.
• Wide stride position with the weight on the front leg.

Possible errors:
Feet touching the floor.

Tip:
To make the exercise more difficult one can "forbid" the compensatory arm movements. A stick or baton makes balancing easier for the 6-7year olds.

Exercise **88**: **Balloon Competition**

■ **Aim:** Improvement of balance
■ **Type:** Partner exercise
■ **Equipment:** One balloon per pair

Starting position:
Upright position opposite each other.

Procedure:
The balloon is to be kept up in the air for as long as possible while the participants stand on one leg or hop.

Possible errors:
Setting down of the leg.

Tip:
The sports instructor indicates when it's time to switch legs.

one leg with one's eyes closed, balancing backwards on the beam, roller skating or on the pedalo. Children with these problems are often over-eager when doing exercises.

A child with obvious coordinative weaknesses requires a lot of praise and understanding from the sports instructor

Children with particularly weak coordinative abilities are recommended to go to special sport therapy or motor therapy. Free access to movement, as well as to sport and games, is extremely important here.

Suitable exercises are therefore described and illustrated on the following pages.

12.1 Exercises for Coordinative Training

Exercise **90: Sideward Hops**

- ■ **Aim:** Coordinative training
- ■ **Type:** Individual exercise
- ■ **Equipment:** None

Starting position:
Upright position, every participant must have a clear view of the sports instructor.

Procedure:
The instructor must demonstrate this exercise, and give a clear explanation to the 6-8year-olds.
The sideward hop is a jump whereby the right leg is brought to the side, and the left arm stretched up in the air at the same time, and then the other way round.

Possible errors:
Using extremities from the same side.

Tip:
Locomotion for young athletes can occur in the following directions: forwards, backwards or sidewards.

Exercise **91: Arms Up**

- ■ **Aim:** Coordinative exercise
- ■ **Type:** Partner exercise
- ■ **Equipment:** Gymnastic ball, one per person

Starting position:
The partners are standing opposite each other, holding their gymnastic ball in both hands.

Procedure:
One leg is set backwards, and at the same time the arms are stretched upwards to the front. The gymnastic balls meet each other in mid-air, and on their way back down again should touch the thighs. Then the other leg is set back.

Possible errors:
Legs must be used in alternation.

Tip:
When each athlete has gotten familiar with the exercise, the pairs can try moving forwards or backwards.
The balls should still touch each other ,however.

Exercise 92: **Bouncing on a Ball**

- ■ **Aim:** Coordinative training
- ■ **Type:** Individual exercise
- ■ **Equipment:** Pezzi balls, one ball per person

Starting position:
All children and adolescents are sitting on a ball.

Procedure:
To get the children used to this exercise, one should start off with foot movements. The children can move from tiptoe position to heel stands for example, whereby one foot is touching the floor with the heel, the other with the toes. Gentle bouncing is the main exercise here, touching the left knee with the right elbow, and the other way round in alternation.

Possible errors:
Moving extremities on the same side.

Tip:
The instructor can determine the tempo by clapping. This makes the exercise easier for many children.

Exercise **93: Road Works**

■ **Aim:** Coordinative training
■ **Type:** Group exercise
■ **Equipment:** Ropes, cones, boxes

Procedure:
The group has to build/lay roads with several ropes. Additional pieces of equipment, such as boxes, can be used as gas stations, or cones as roadwork boundaries. The children should drive along these streets at their own individual tempo.
Various forms of locomotion are possible here:
• Walking and running (driving in first gear and fast driving).
• Walking backwards (the cars roll down a hill backwards).
• Hopping on one leg (the cars have a flat tire).
• Slalom around the cones (driving to the boundaries of the roadwork) etc.

Possible errors:
Treading on the ropes.

Tip:
This exercise is particularly suitable for 6-8-year-olds.

Exercise 94: Who Has the Most Apples in Their Basket?

■ **Aim:** Coordinative training
■ **Type:** Group exercise
■ **Equipment:** Two boxes and gymnastic balls

Starting position:
Two groups are formed. They are standing behind a suitable marked boundary around the upturned boxes.

Procedure:
The participants have to try, and throw as many balls into the box within a particular time limit (e.g. 2 minutes).

Possible errors:
The boundary is not adhered to.

Tip:
Depending on the group's performance ability, it is also possible to use tennis balls, or even balloons for this exercise.

Exercise **95: Pedalo Rides**

- ■ **Aim:**   Coordinative training
- ■ **Type:**   Partner exercise
- ■ **Equipment:** Pedalos (as many as are available), batons

Starting position:
Upright position at the narrow end of the room.

Procedure:
For a group who have never used the pedalo, it's necessary to have a partner who walks along beside the child on the pedalo.
Here are a few examples of what one can do with this piece of equipment.

- It's a good idea to start off with small movements, such as practicing one revolution. The feet end up in the same position that they started in. One can then try riding backwards.
- Using two batons as walking sticks, one proceeds as follows: When setting the right leg forward, one sets down the left "walking stick" to the front etc.
- A further variation, which requires a high level of coordination, involves the same technique with leg and trunk. The walking stick is held at chest height. If the right leg is to the front, then the left shoulder or the left side of the stick should also come to the front.
- The sports instructor can interrupt the flowing forward and backward riding with sudden claps.

Possible errors:
Setting the right leg and right arm forward at the same time.

Tip:
Pedalos are a popular source of variety with all ages.
Another good and popular form of coordinative training is with the skipping rope. See exercise 24 Chapter 7.2)

13 PERCEPTION – PHYSICAL AND SPATIAL ORIENTATION

Perceiving, perception is a general comprehensive term for the process of gaining information through physical and environmental stimuli, including the emotional processes involved in this and the modification that occurs based on experience and thinking. (E.J. KIPHARD 1996).

The following example of the body's perception may help to clarify the facts here:

You're standing upright, your feet are as far apart from each other as your hips, your arms relaxed. Slowly shift your weight to the front, lifting your heels from the floor in the process. You're standing on the balls of your feet, and now try to find your balance.

Choose a fixed point in front of you, check your balance again, and then close your eyes. Concentrate, be at one with yourself, and wait and see what happens.

After several seconds open your eyes, and stand ap again on the floor.

Perception is how you have just sensed the orientation of your own body, and the orientation in the room.

A person who is unable to orientate himself via his own body or within a room, has a disturbed sense of perception, and cannot move normally for this reason.

The gift of orientation is partly inherent, and partly acquired. It develops alongside a child's ability to sit himself up, to stand up, and to move around. A 4-5 year-old child should, for example, be able to understand the terms "above" and "below" and implement them correctly. When a child is six he should be able to differentiate "right" from "left".

Athletes in general take in their bodies more intensively than those who don't do any sports; they pay attention to their ability of movement, and state of condition. Their body perception and body awareness is obviously better developed than that of a person who lives a life with little movement and exercise.

With every movement, the brain receives a large amount of kinesthetic (sensing the movement) responses and feedback from the muscles and joints, as well as one's sense of balance in the inner ear. If the brain receives only minor kinesthetic responses due to disturbances or lack of movement, this can result in a weakness of one's body scheme.

Children with a weakness in their body scheme also lack an optical overview; they register irrelevant trivial things while missing out on the important matters. They find it difficult to pay attention to several things simultaneously and, because of this, these children only learn slowly that the human body is made up of individual pieces, and what form it takes in its entirety (E. J. KIPHARD 1996).

Weaknesses in body scheme occur more frequently among children than previously assumed.

Examples of such weaknesses are:
- Difficulties getting dressed (buttoning the wrong way, shoes on the wrong feet).
- Mixing up "up" and "down".
- Mixing up "front" and "back".
- Mixing up "right" and "left".
- Mixing up limbs and parts of the body (lifting up the whole leg when supposed to be moving the feet).

The following little exercises can be assigned for homework: puffing up their cheeks, pressing out their stomachs, touching their earlobe with their little finger, touching their left knee with their right hand with their eyes open and then closed.

Perception exercises within a group are suitable at the end of a gymnastics session as a calm atmosphere is required for the majority of these exercises.

13.1 Exercises for Perception

Exercise 96: Hidden Monument

- **Aim:** Improvement of body perception
- **Type:** Group exercise
- **Equipment:** Swing sheet or blanket (one blanket per group)
  For children over eight, a sheet as well

Starting position:
The children and adolescents are divided up into groups of three, four or five depending on the size of the total group.

Procedure:
One group member is the "monument", and hides under the sheet or blanket, and assumes a particular position (whatever he feels like). This position is not allowed to be changed after the start signal. The other members of the group try to find out what this position is by touching and feeling the "monument", and get into the same position. After all children are in position, the instructor removes the blanket saying, "Open monument." and then selects a winner by comparing the "monument" and the other group members; the child with the closest similarity to the monument is the winner. In the next round he is then the "hidden monument".

Possible errors:
Peeking under the blanket.

Tip:
When doing this exercise with teens, it's a good idea to blindfold the other group members!

Exercise **97**: **Patience**

■ **Aim:**   Improvement of body perception
■ **Type:**   Partner exercise
■ **Equipment:** Clothes pins (at least five per pair)

Starting position:
A child or adolescent is lying in prone position with his eyes closed; his partner is sitting down beside him.

Procedure:
The child sitting down tries to clip clothes pins onto child B's clothes without him noticing. If he does notice, he must say where it is, e.g. right shoulder, back, left foot etc. Child A must then remove them again. If B gives a wrong answer, or has not noticed a clothes pin being clipped on, the clothes peg remains where it is. The aim is to clip on as many clothes pins as possible.

Possible errors:
The child lying down opens his eyes!

Tip:
A high level of concentration is required for this exercise, and is therefore suitable for restless and hyperactive children.

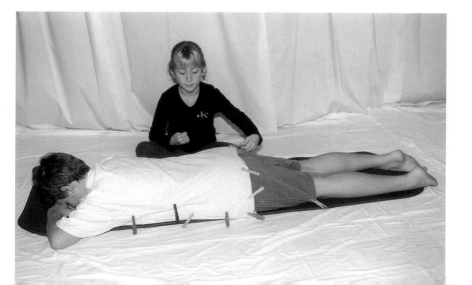

Exercise **98**: **Space Games**

- ■ **Aim:**   Improvement of body perception
- ■ **Type:**   Group exercise
- ■ **Equipment:** Hoops (one hoop per person)

Starting position:
Each participant receives a hoop (planet) which is laid on the floor.

Procedure:
The children are "space ships", and run around the "planets" throughout the room (universe) with their arms stretched out to the side.

A: The sports instructor claps his hands, and each child picks out a hoop (planet), and jumps inside. This is a practice exercise for exercise B.

B: Now the children have to place parts of the body into the hoops together. The instructor gives e.g. the following commands: five feet or three elbows or three shoulders or seven hands etc. The children must get the right number of parts into the hoops or onto the "planet".

Tip:
This exercise can be made more interesting for teens with commands such as three feet and 17 fingers at the same time.

Exercise 99: Creative Line

- **Aim:** Improvement of body perception and sensitivity
- **Type:** Group exercise
- **Equipment:** None

Starting position:
Approx. five children are sitting behind each other with their legs stretched out.

Procedure:
The person at the back begins to draw letters, numbers, or a simple object on the back of the person sitting in front of him who, without saying anything, continues this drawing, and so on, until it reaches the person at the front. The first and last person compare verbally what message was being passed on. The person at the back now moves to the very front for the next round.

Possible errors:
Conversation during the exercise is not allowed, as concentration and a quiet atmosphere are required here.

Tip:
In order to alter this exercise after a while, it is also possible to "roll" the drawings onto the back of the person in front by using a small ball or spiky ball.

Exercise 100: Leading the Blind

- **Aim:** Improvement of spatial perception
- **Type:** Partner exercise
- **Equipment:** Hoops and scarves (one hoop and scarf per pair)

Starting position:
One child is blindfolded, and is the "blind man". He climbs into the hoop, and holds it at stomach height while his partner does the leading.

Procedure:
The child leading the "blind man" sends impulses through the hoop (careful pull to the right and left). Walking slowly around the room the "blind man" should try to orientate himself as well as possible, so that he always knows exactly where he is. He should be able to answer questions about their current position, e.g. where the window or room is, by pointing in that particular direction.

Possible errors:
Walking too quickly as spatial orientation loses out then.

Tip:
This exercise can be made more difficult for teens, when the "blind man" is slowly turned around occasionally, or led backwards.

14 SAMPLE EXERCISE PROGRAMS

	Kids 6-8 years	Big Kids 9-11 years	Teens 12-14 years
Materials	Gymnastic balls ropes batons one box clothes pins papers with animal names (doubled)	Gymnastic balls ropes balls one medical ball wall of bars boxes pedalos scarves sheets or blankets (max. 5)	Gymnastic balls ropes batons hoops pezzi balls scarves long benches
Warm-up	Imitating animals, copying figures, rattles and scarves	Running and walking games, partner exercises with balloons and balls, music	Current chart music combined with step combinations (aerobics, hip-hop)
Exercises Foot and lower leg muscles	Ex. 4: "Flycatching frogs" Ex. 12: "Children of stone"	Ex.1: "Toe figures" Ex. 7: "Windscreen wipers" Ex. 11: "Partner support"	Ex. 3: "Caterpillar" Ex. 6: "Sawing exercises" Ex. 10: "Push up stretching"

	Kids 6-8 years	Big Kids 9-11 years	Teens 12-14 years
Leg and hip muscles	Ex. 16: "Stuck Together" Ex. 21: "Walking the Dog" Ex. 24: "Skipping Rope in Many Variations" Ex. 25: "Snake Hunting" Ex. 29: "Circling the Body" Ex. 41: "Hands of the Clock"	Ex. 17: "Target Throwing" Ex. 24: "Rope Skipping in Many Variations" Ex. 27: "Kneeling position at the Wall" Ex. 31: "Leg Up" Ex. 33: "Drawing on the Wall" Ex. 36: "Butterfly" Ex. 42: "Leg to the Stomach"	Ex. 13: "Wall Sliding" Ex. 18: "Trees in the Wind" Ex. 22. "Leg Presses" Ex. 28: "Who Can Stay Standing on One Leg for the Longest?" Ex. 30: "Press the Ball against the Wall" Ex. 34: "Partner Roll" Ex. 38: "Right and Left" Ex. 43: "Leg to the Front and Out to the Side"
Trunk muscles	Ex. 47: "Creeping Dog" Ex. 54: "Beetle on his Back" Ex. 56: "Runway" Ex. 57: "Man in the Moon" Ex: 61: "Parcel"	Ex. 48: "Who Has no Balloons?" Ex. 50: "Rubberband" Ex. 52: "Bike Tour" Ex. 58: "Tightening the Bow"	Ex. 46: "Roll the Ball" Ex. 55: "Throwing the Ball" Ex. 59: "Stretching in Pairs"

	Kids 6-8 years	Big Kids 9-11 years	Teens 12-14 Years
Shoulder and arm muscles	Ex. 65: "Wheelbarrow Race" Ex. 72: "Thirsty Cat" Ex. 79: "Submarine"	Ex. 65: "Wheelbarrow Race" Ex. 68: "Let the Ball Hop" Ex. 72: "Thirsty Cat" Ex. 73: "Stretching at the Wall"	Ex. 64: "Matching Strength" Ex. 67: "Bascule Bridge" Ex. 71: "Let Yourself Hang" Ex. 76: "Partner Stretching"
Muscles of the whole body	Ex. 83: "Salamander"	Ex. 80: "Feet Together"	Ex. 81: "Mini Push ups" Ex. 82: "Diagonal Stretching"
Exercises for balance training	Ex. 87: "Walking the Rope"	Ex. 88: "Balloon Competition"	Ex. 85: "Gymnasts"
Exercises for coordinative training	Ex. 94: "Who Has the Most Apples in his Basket?"	Ex. 95: "Pedalo Rides"	Ex. 92: "Bouncing on a Ball"
End section	Community game "Meet Your Match" or chasing game "Pluck a Chuck", see Chapter 15	Community game "Detectives" or competitive game "Wandering Medicine Ball", see Chapter 15	Community game "Hip hep" (bouncing the ball), see Chapter 15
Relaxation phase	Ex. 97: "Patience"	Ex. 96: "Hidden Monument"	Ex. 100:"Leading the Blind"

15 GAMES WITH THAT EXTRA SOMETHING

Here are a few examples for community, team, and chasing games which, apart from their basic gymnastic functions, guarantee that fun and pleasure can always be included.

Community Games

Hoop Hunting:

The group is standing in a circle, each participant holding his neighbour's hands. The sports instructor hangs a hoop on two participants' arms. The hunt begins: one hoop must hunt the other one, and this is only possible when every group member climbs through the hoop, and passes it on in this way without letting the hands go.

Detectives:

The entire group walks, crawls, hops through the room until the trainer claps, and freezes all participants to stone. Two children or adolescents are elected to be detectives, and have to take a careful look at every single group member, and try to remember their position.

The detectives then go out of the room for a brief moment while three "frozen" participants change their position. The detectives appear in the room again, and have to try, and find these three children.

Another variation of this game is to swap places with another child rather than being frozen to stone.

Meet your Match:

The trainer distributes little pieces of paper, all of which are pairs. The pictures on them are types of animals e.g. snakes, horses, pigs, cows, birds, frogs and spiders. Matchmaking begins as the pairs go around the room trying to find each other without speaking, but by making the typical animal noises only.

Mirror Game:

In order to start off this game with an easy version, two children sit opposite each other. One child carries out certain movements – whatever he feels like – while his partner gives its reflection by imitating these movements. For a more advanced version, one can move on to "higher" starting positions, such as the knee stand or upright position, or alternatively the group size is increased to four children.

Hip, Hep:

When playing this game, it is important to take the different age groups into consideration although it obviously depends on the individual performance capacity of each group. With 6-9-year-olds, however, it's advisable to start off in a sitting position. Each child receives a ball; "hip" means right; "hep" means left.

The trainer gives the above commands and each child must roll or pass his ball to the partner on his right or left. For the 9-14-year-olds, one starts off standing up. The ball can be passed, thrown or bounced to the right or left.

Sounds:

The entire group is blindfolded. The sports instructor claps his hands, whistles, or drums from a particular corner of the room. The participants must now point their arms out in the direction the sound is coming from. An advanced version is to try and find where the instructor is.

Vegetable Market

All participants stand in line behind one another holding on to the waist of the child in front, except for one child. The child at the front holds onto the wall of bars, and is the market seller. The child outside the line is the customer. Customer and seller hold the following conversation:

" Would you sell me an onion?" – " Yes of course, try plucking one!".

Now the customer tries to pull another child out of the line. As soon as he has got hold of an onion (child), he goes to the end of the line, and the "onion" is now the customer.

It is very important that the children do not merely hold on to the shirt of the child in front.

Team Games
"Wandering Medicine Ball"

The participants are divided up into two groups, both groups are a few meters away from each other, and each group is standing behind a marking (e.g. long bench). In the middle of the playing field is a medicine ball, which has to be brought over to the other side. Every participant has a gymnastic ball in his hand, and by aiming at the medicine ball tries to get it to move until it reaches the other team's boundary area. This is often teamwork here, as some athletes are good throwers, and fast runners are needed for picking up all the balls.

"Reptile Rally"

Two teams are formed, half of which are on all fours behind a marking, and several meters away from each other. The participants in the rally are the "reptiles", characterized by a sand sack on their backs. After the sports instructor has given a start signal, the reptiles start crawling to the other side as quickly as possible where the next "reptiles" are waiting for their run.

However, if the sand sack falls onto the floor, the "reptile" must go back and repeat his run. The rally is finshed when all children have been "reptiles" once.

"Snail Trail"

Two giant snails are marked out on the floor, either with chalk or sticky tape, and each snail is divided up in squares. A stone (or similar object) is at the beginning of each snail.

The group divides into two teams, and these get into a row behind the snails. When the start signal has been given, the participants must hop on one leg, moving the stone into each square towards the finish, and without the stone going outside the lines. The finish is at the other end of the snail, and the stone is laid back to the beginning again for the second team member. If a participant makes a mistake, such as skipping a square or going outside the lines, then he must start again from the beginning.

Chasing Games

"Growing Snake"

The sports instructor picks out a pair to be the "snake", and these are joined at the hand for the entire game. All other participants have to be careful now as the "snake" has to catch or touch them. Each child that is touched has to hang on to the "snake" by one hand, and thus help to catch the other children until nobody else is running around.

"Chain Game"

Depending on the size of the group, approximately six children should get together, and hold each other's hands. The first chain link must try, and catch the last link although the chain must not break in the middle.

"Pluck a Chuck"

One child is the "chicken" with clothes pins clipped onto his T-shirt. When a sign has been given, the other players try to pluck the chicken by removing the clothes pins without holding onto him. After the "chicken" has been fully plucked, the clothes pins are then counted to see who is the winner.

"Hunting Hares"

One member of the group is the hunter while the rest of the group is hares. The "hunter" tries to hit the "hares" with a ball. Bouncing the ball is allowed. The "hare" that has been caught now becomes a "hunter", too, and the game continues like this until there are no more hares left. The "hunters" must try and hit the body, and the "hares" are allowed to protect themselves with their arms.

"Tails"

Each participant attaches a scarf, handkerchief or Thera-band® to the waist of his pants at the back. All children now try to take each other's tails while running about. Anyone who loses his scarf has lost; the winner is the person with the most "tails" at the end.

"Bear, Are You Awake?"

One group member is the bear who is rolled up asleep in a corner of the hall and snoring. The other children ask him quietly, "Bear, are you awake?". The bear continues to snore loudly, and the children ask the question again, a little bit louder this time, but the bear is still asleep. Now the children call out loud, "Bear, are you awake?", and suddenly the "bear" gets up, and runs about after the other children, trying to tag them. Those children that have been touched are also "bears" in the next round; they sleep in the corner, and try to catch the other children.

16 SOME WORDS OF ADVICE IN THE CASE OF SPORT INJURIES

A sports instructor who is assigned a group of children and adolescents should also be prepared when it comes to a sports accident, or even only a small injury. Luckily enough, functional gymnastics is not a form of sports with a high accidental rate compared to, for example football, skiing, handball or tennis.

However, it is very important not to immediately break out in a panic when an accident does happen; keeping one's bearings is what counts here, so as to be able to help the child immediately, both calmly, and with the necessary basic knowledge.

Note:
I am not a doctor, and am not qualified to give professional medical advice. I have treated patients with sports accidents after the doctor's diagnosis and treatment. Therefore, the information and advice that follow is based on personal practical experience in the sports field. Needless to say, should any doubts arise regarding an injury, it is essential that professional medical advice is sought, and a doctor is consulted.

16.1 Emergency Measures

Luckily enough, the injuries that occur in the gymnastic field are mostly **closed injuries**. These are injuries without any wounds to the skin, and are generally caused by blunt injuries such as:

■ Bruising	(contusion)
■ Muscle-tendon-ligament strain	(distortion)
■ Dislocation	(luxation)
■ Muscle-tendon-ligament tearing	(rupture)
■ Bone break	(fracture)

With these so-called closed injuries, a certain plan of treatment has proven to be successful.

Break:	■	Discontinue sports activity, examination
	■	Rest
	■	No stretching, no massage, and no heat treatment
Ice:	■	To ease the pain, to minimize bruising and swelling
	■	A period of 15-20 minutes is recommended, for ice treatments, however, only 2-5 minutes
	■	Use of cold tap water, cold packs, ice-pops, ice cubes, or compression bandage with iced water
Compression:	■	To reduce swelling
	■	Moderate tautness of pressure bandages only, no cutting off circulation!
	■	Place wet-cold bandages or cold packs over the bandage
Keep it Up :	■	Also to reduce swelling
	■	The injured part of the body is kept up

When dealing with **open injuries,** however, one should follow the procedures below when offering emergency aid.

Open injuries should be looked after immediately, i.e. cleaned, disinfected and covered with a sterile bandage or compress. If it is quite a large injury, or if there is a foreign body in the wound, one should cover the injury with a sterile bandage, and seek a doctor immediately.

In these days of AIDS and hepatitis B, wearing disposable plastic gloves when in contact with blood and saliva should be a matter of course for a sports instructor.

In the case of **particular injuries**, such as *injuries to the spine*, suitable medical transport must be organized. The patient should stay flat while waiting.

Concussion can occur after a *head injury* or hit on the head. This often goes hand in hand with unconsciousness, vomiting and a loss of memory. One proceeds as with the spinal injury except that the head must be raised here.

In the case of a *fracture,* one should place the fractured area in a splint, keep it still, and cool it if possible before seeking a doctor.

If *nose bleeding* occurs, the patient must stay in upright position, and with the head in normal position. It's a good idea to hold the nose closed for several minutes, and spit out surplus blood, rather than swallowing it.

16.2 Consequences of Overstrain

The **factors responsible for overstrain** and sports injuries can be an inadequate training state, physical conditions of fatigue e.g. after an influenza infection, injuries which are not fully healed, and nutritional or electrolyte deficiencies.

Outer causes of this are inadequate sports equipment, bad overall conditions such as ground surface, sports equipment or outside influence as in a foul.

Muscle soreness is a symptom of overstrain which is probably familiar to everyone. Temporary muscle soreness is due to both lactic acid deposits in muscle tissue, as well as fine muscle fiber rupture. Pain occurs under pressure, or when stretched between 8-24 hours after being overstrained, which in turn causes a reduction in muscle strength. One should cut down the training intensity until the soreness has passed. A preventative measure here is to choose short training phases, and low intensity before taking on an unfamiliar load.

Another painful symptom is a muscle cramp, which mostly turns up during or after an extreme load. This particularly affects calf and thigh muscles. An inadequate state of training is the main cause of this, as well as an **extreme loss of fluids and electrolytes or circulation problems**. Suitable emergency measures here are careful stretching of the painful muscles, and activation of the counteractive muscles, as this all helps to relax the cramps. In the case of a cramp in the calf muscle, one must tense the foot lifting muscles; a cramp in the rear thigh muscles can be alleviated by tensing the front thigh muscles, i.e. by stretching one's leg.

Pulling, fiber rupture and tearing of the muscles occurs as a result of **muscle fatigue** or a **metabolic disturbance**. Rapidly increasing cramp-like pains are a sign of a pulled muscle; whereas sharp, piercing pains indicate tearing of the muscle, and this leads to a complete stop in the movement processes. Typical for all three cases is an initial "protective posture" followed by pain under pressure, under tension, and when stretched, as well as bruising (hematoma development). A doctor should be consulted immediately.

Most consequences of overstraining can be avoided with the following three steps:
- **A suitable warm-up**
- **Training appropriate to performance capacity**
- **A balanced diet**

The importance of warming up, and doing training that fits in with one's performance level has been dealt with in detail in the previous chapters. The next chapter gives a brief explanation of healthy nutrition, a topic which can also be discussed with children and adolescents, e.g. in the finishing phases of a lesson.

17 IMPORTANT PRINCIPLES FOR NUTRITION

Balanced and healthy nutrition is just as important for one's well being as physical training. Healthy eating and drinking can be an interesting experience even for children and adolescents; however, it should still be tackled in a playful manner with these age groups.

Food's main task should be to provide the body with the energy it needs to build up and maintain tissue and organs. The body must be supplied with nutrients, vitamins and minerals as it needs these for growth and solid bones, as well as for hair and skin.

Nutrients include proteins, carbohydrates, fats, minerals, vitamins and trace elements.

Proteins:
- They are the body's most important building components.
- They are the building materials for muscles, skin, organs and connective tissue.
- We can eat animal proteins, e.g. meat, fish, eggs, milk, cheese.
- As well as proteins of vegetable origin, such as cereals, pulse vegetables, corn, beans and bread.

Carbohydrates or sugar:
- These supply and store energy.
- Carbohydrates are to be found in all starchy products such as potatoes, cereals and pastries.
- Carbohydrates supply the body with a constant flow of energy; pure sugar, on the other hand, causes blood sugar fluctuations and therefore an increased appetite.

Fats:
- We need these for energy during endurance performances, as a fat reserve for bad times, as well as cushioning of the body surface.
- Vegetable fats are present in nuts or oils; animal fats are in meat, fish, sausage meat and dairy products.

Minerals: ───────────────────────
■ We need minerals for muscle and nerve function, as well as for the build-up of bones.
■ They are divided up into calcium, potassium, sodium and magnesium.
■ As calcium requirements increase with age, it is important to eat dairy products regularly.
■ Potassium is essential for muscle cell activities, and is present in bananas.
■ We take in a lot of sodium in the form of table salt.
■ Regular sports activity often leads to magnesium deficiency, and therefore, also to muscle cramps. These can be combatted with cereals, vegetables and cheese.

Vitamins: ───────────────────────
Vitamins are substances which the body cannot produce itself, and which we therefore, have to take in through our diet.
■ Vitamins can be divided up into water-soluble and fat-soluble vitamins.
■ The B- and C- vitamins belong to the water-soluble group, and we must take these in regularly as the body can only store them in very small amounts. They are present in fruit, vegetables, salad, cereals, meat and dairy products.
■ The fat-soluble vitamins A,D, E, F and K can be stored in the liver, and are present in vegetables, milk, meat and fish.

Trace elements: ───────────────────────
■ The body requires trace elements in very small portions only.
■ The body is supplied with trace elements through our diet, e.g. iron, and via air or drinking water, e.g. iodine.
■ Iron is considered to be the most important trace element; an iron deficiency leads to tiredness and paleness.

It is advisable to cut down on those foods which can have a damaging effect on our bodies when taken in large amounts. These wrongdoers are unfortunately mostly very popular among children and adolescents such as fats, sugars, salt, and in some cases caffeine. There is nothing wrong with moderate amounts of these foods; however, one should not, for example, eat fatty fast food daily or consume large amounts of sweets every day.